SELECTED ENGLISH CLASSICS
General Editor: A. H. R. Ball, M.A.

SELECTIONS FROM WORDSWORTH

SELECTIONS FROM

Wordsworth

Edited with Notes and an Introduction
by
PHILIP WAYNE, M.A.
Headmaster of St Marylebone Grammar School

GINN AND COMPANY LTD.
QUEEN SQUARE, LONDON, W.C.1

GINN AND COMPANY LTD.

All Rights Reserved

053502

Printed in Great Britain
by Turnbull & Spears, Edinburgh

PREFACE

IN preparing this book, I have made my choice of Wordsworth's poems not so much for their celebrity or literary history as for their poetic ardour. This principle has excluded several stock pieces wherein, to my mind, the poet's inspiration was cold, or he was writing in vindication of his poetic tenets rather than with the compelling emotion that inspires his best work.

The Introduction has been written in the conviction that Wordsworth, though he embodied the spirit of his Age, is yet one of the individual giants in English poetry, and must be seen in his own strong originality rather than as the leader of a Movement. Bearing in mind that readers may arrive prejudiced by Wordsworth's moralising pieces, I have tried, even in the small space I had, to give an outline or impression of his full stature. Here, and in the Notes, I am indebted to many writers; particularly to those named in the "Guide to Reading."

Wordsworth is not easy—poets of transcendental imagination rarely are—and if I have left some difficulties undisguised, I am comforted by the notion that most people would rather have difficulties than editorial condescension. I trust, at any rate, that what I have written will in no way stand between the reader and the fresh joy of Wordsworth's best work. Readers who accept his poetry with growing trust will be entering into a part of our English heritage such as may, in troubled times, serve them with courage and clear sight.

P. W.

LONDON, 1932

CONTENTS

(In the text, the titles in italics are those supplied by the Editor)

SELECTIONS FROM *THE PRELUDE*—*continued*

LYRICAL POEMS :

INTRODUCTION

I. THE APPROACH TO WORDSWORTH

WORDSWORTH grew up in freedom, loved Nature passionately, suffered for liberty, and, after work of superb genius,
settled down to a long, quiet life. His eighty years included
an epoch of crisis and upheaval in the history of mankind
(he was nineteen when the French Revolution broke out),
and his own inner story was more than once involved in
emotional storms that shook the ground of his strong being.
There is therefore a great deal of him to be taken into
account in trying to answer that basic question that under-
lies every discussion of every great poet : namely, how does
his poetry spring from his life ?

Some say that all art is valuable in so far as it gives the key
to the soul of the man creating it. Others represent art as a
mysterious bloom that flourishes apart from the actual life of
its creator, remote in fact from any ' corruption that inhabits
his frail blood.' The first view ignores the superiority by
which a man's art can surpass and outlast his life ; the second
exalts that superiority with such enthusiasm as to lose sight
of any intimate connection between life, untidy and im-
perfect as we know it, and art, whose selective power
removes it to a sphere of permanence above the blurred
continuity of personal history.

The life of Wordsworth was girt with an altogether extraordinary power of joy ; it also comprised times of difficulty,
of dismay, of temper, awkwardness, and even of dulness.
To view steadily his supreme achievements together with his
peculiar failures is to come to a sane conclusion upon the

nature of poetry : it surely must be the outcome of those rare moments, more or less sustained, when a human spirit works the material of its life under the fire of imaginative ecstasy to a passionate justness of proportion. Such a perfection as this we call beauty, and the sublime proportion strikes us as having a truth beyond our human limitations, partaking therefore of immortality. Thus, said Wordsworth, " Poetry is the breath and finer spirit of all knowledge." If, through that finer spirit, a man achieves one sublimation of some feature or aspect of his life, he writes one great poem ; but he is only a great poet in so far as that achievement is his frequently or sustainedly. In this sense Wordsworth is, with Shakespeare and Milton, among the few greatest of our English poets. By the side of his best work, profound and lovely and enduring as it is, his failures pale to insignificance and almost to irrelevance. Yet there was in Wordsworth a certain stiffness of character which allowed him sometimes to persist in un-inspired poems and rendered him, particularly in later life, liable to faults of egotism. Moreover, as he grew older, he laid more and more stress on the poet's function as a teacher ; and so, generations of pious persons have put upon children his least inspired work as moral pabulum, while they them-selves, missing the glorious freshness of Wordsworth's best things, have sought in him, particularly in times when belief seemed defeated by science, for ready-made philosophic or religious comfort.[1]

This moralising tradition of Wordsworth, supported by the

[1] For instance, the sickly *Pet Lamb*, with the apostrophe " Drink, pretty creature, drink ! " was for years staple diet in elementary schools, while the grown-up seekers impressed at least one great Wordsworthian, Matthew Arnold, very sadly : "a great room in one of our dismal pro-vincial towns ; dusty air and jaded afternoon daylight ; benches full of men with bald heads and women in spectacles ; an orator lifting up his face . . . to declaim . . . lines of Wordsworth ; and in the soul of any poor child of nature who may have wandered thither, an unutterable sense of lamentation, and mourning, and woe ! "

least attractive features of the poet's own work and character, still stands in the way of many people's approach to his true greatness. " We hate," said the young Keats, " poetry that has a palpable design upon us." And any editor trying to give a faithful picture in a short space may well fear that some oddity or egotism of Wordsworth's, truthfully rendered, may stick too readily in a young reader's mind, while the more difficult envisagement of poetic grandeur suffers thereby. Yet Shakespeare may have had chilblains—at any rate, he sympathised with the 'kibed heel'—and Professor Garrod says rightly, in his book on Wordsworth : " We are entitled to all the talk, small and great, about great poets, which we can scrape together, with this proviso : that we can, and do, relate it to the primary fact about them, namely, that they *are* great." Some such resolution is particularly desirable in the approach to Wordsworth, for we have possibly to banish a very false image by which, says the same writer, " for something like a century the understanding of his poetry has been vitiated." Fairness and modesty demand a clean start ; so do one's own enjoyment and gain. " Sir," said the Curator at the National Gallery, to a visitor who had spoken slightingly of the pictures, " it is not the pictures that are on trial here, it is you."

II. BIOGRAPHICAL OUTLINE

Early Life

William Wordsworth, son of a country law-agent, was born in 1770 at Cockermouth in Cumberland. He was the second of five children. Dorothy, his celebrated sister, was a year younger. They had three brothers. There was racial strength in those Wordsworths. John became a sea-captain and Christopher the Master of Trinity, Cambridge : these had their trials of scholarship and of the sea ; but their brother's victories of the mind, held fast in poetry, were destined for enduring fame. Their mother died when William was nearly eight. He remembered her tenderly ; indeed he was the one over whom she had been anxious. " He will be remarkable," she said, " either for good or for evil." Wordsworth says of himself, " I was of a stiff, moody, and violent temper " ; and, although he was to become the poet of peace, of " joy in widest commonalty spread," he was to keep his toughness and independence of spirit to the end.

The freedom of his early childhood received no set-back in his schooldays at Hawkshead (1778-87). Young Wordsworth liked his work and his master, and he learnt a fair amount of Latin and Mathematics. Those days were " very happy ones," he says, " chiefly because I was left at liberty . . . to read whatever books I liked. For instance, I read all Fielding's works, *Don Quixote, Gil Blas*, and any part of Swift that I liked." Moreover, he did not live at the School, but with a good old cottage-dame, and the boys had extraordinary freedom to range both early and late the woods and hills about their lovely lake of Esthwaite. " Fair seed-time had my soul," writes Wordsworth, and indeed, for a joyous spirit of freedom it would be hard to find the equal of his school, then or now. The delights, of fireside or of forest, enjoyed by his " noisy crew " are told in *The Prelude, or The Growth of a Poet's Mind* : it is there also that we must seek for an understanding of the wakening and unfolding with which sheer, passionate love of nature led him first to reflective percipience of nature's lovelinesses as " types of a majestic intellect," and finally to the superb joy of feeling that man's mind is the arch-collaborator in such beauty, becoming even half-creator by that imaginative power. The most extensive biographies [1] are no match for *The Prelude* or *Tintern Abbey* in following these processes. The present little account must

---

[1] See pages 198-200.

be content with a quick review of leading traits and influences in the poet's life.

Wordsworth's father died during the boy's school-time. Relatives took charge of the young Wordsworths, from now " squandered abroad," as Dorothy says, and in 1787 William was sent, with the help of an uncle, to Cambridge. He read what he liked, loved the lingering memories of past poets and thinkers, disliked the church element, and revisited his native hills with growing poetic ardour. Instead of reading hard in his final vacation he went for a walking tour across France to Switzerland, doing 350 miles in fourteen days. In poetry he was not yet fledged, but he had more than once felt a power of inner dedication.

Indecisive months followed his meagre finish at Cambridge. Full of energy but lacking aim, he returned to France, and this second visit (1791-92) was to be most important in his history. First, friendship with a distinguished French patriot, Michel Beaupuy, focused his sympathies upon the Revolution ; and the spectacle of Man, his destiny and his affections, now began to supersede the importance of Nature in the poet's mind. Secondly, he experienced, in Orleans, a serious love affair, the existence of which was not known outside Wordsworth's family circle until over a hundred years afterwards ; nor is it likely that the inner significance of the story will ever be understood, for the poet has left no record of what his feelings were.

The young poet accepted the Revolution as natural and necessary. Rousseau's advocacy of a return to natural conditions appealed to him without need of doctrinaire theory : he had grown up in freedom among dalesmen, and he wished for no finer types. His republican enthusiasm now mounted to the danger of his life and career.[1] He joined radical Friends of the Revolution in London and wrote powerfully in the

[1] See page 27.

cause.[1] It was, then, to him a heartrending turn of history
when radical opinion was overwhelmed, and England turned
definitely against France. War was declared in February,
1793. Wordsworth, whose nature was as English as it
was loyal, knew for a time the bitterness of exulting in
English defeat.[2] His relatives very naturally discarded him :
he had no occupation and no prospects, and what principles
he had seemed to them odious. To endure such a position
in attachment to a glorious cause is tolerable ; but terror-
ridden France turned presently to inglorious aggression, so
that Wordsworth's hopes seemed doomed to mockery and
despair. Transplanted from his native hills and baffled by
humanity's failures, his mind sought refuge in Godwin's
alluring gospel of salvation by pure reason. Both the pre-
judices of tradition and the bonds of contract were to be dissolved in the application of Reason to each problem as it
arose. This doctrine, ignoring human passions, and remote
from that concrete reality of nature and of men which was
the base of Wordsworth's power, was bound eventually to
leave the poet worse off than before. His four years after
leaving Cambridge (January, 1791) seemed to have culmin-
ated in dismay. Nevertheless, it would be false to imagine
him as a romantic figure of poetic gloom ; rather is he to be
pictured as a self-willed northerner, not very communicative
about his woes, obscure in his aims and movements, dis-
tressed in his racial good-sense to be thought a ne'er-do-well,
and unshaken as to his own poetic vocation.

Middle Period : highest Poetic Activity

In 1795 came the great turning-point of Wordsworth's life.
He was able, thanks to a small legacy, to settle down in the
country, united at last with his sister, whose faith in him

---

[1] *A Letter to the Bishop of Llandaff*, not published, however, until 1876.
[2] Cf. *The Prelude*, x. 284-99.

had never wavered. The healing power of Dorothy's presence, and of their shared delight in the common sights of rustic life, was of incalculable blessing to Wordsworth. At first the poet lingered upon rural beauty

> and rejoiced
> To lay the inner faculties asleep.[1]

But Dorothy's quiet good faith and extraordinary sensitiveness gradually worked in gentlest admonition :

> for, though bedimmed and changed
> Much, as it seemed, I was no further changed
> Than as a clouded and a waning moon :
> She whispered still that brightness would return,
> She, in the midst of all, preserved me still
> A Poet, made me seek beneath that name,
> And that alone, my office upon earth.[2]

Dorothy's fervent love of nature was joined with a free kindliness towards peasants and travellers, and this helped Wordsworth in his reconciliation of the figure of man with its enduring background of nature. A time had begun

> When every day brought with it some new sense
> Of exquisite regard for common things.

The same eventful autumn brought Wordsworth the friendship of Coleridge. Brilliant, unpractical, generous Coleridge was to have profound influence on his brother poet for years. " Perhaps, indeed," says Professor Garrod, " Coleridge's greatest work is Wordsworth—and, like all his other work, Coleridge left it unfinished." To guard against exaggeration, however, it must be remembered that, splendid as was the mental stimulus from Coleridge, the Wordsworths had just entered upon a unison both of life and of outlook, natural to them and never to be shaken, though the character of Coleridge wavered into disintegration. Dorothy's was the

---

[1] *The Prelude*, xii. 146. [2] *Ibid.*, xi. 342-48.

slighter voice ; and maybe if Coleridge had not, fifteen years
later, become estranged, Wordsworth might have been saved
from some of the narrowness of his later life ; but that unison
was in the peculiar Wordsworthian mode, and it produced
his best work, as well as his worst.

Wordsworth and Coleridge : *momentous Friendship and Work*

Even as Beaupuy had helped the young Wordsworth to
political definition of his vague sympathies with mankind, so
Coleridge's philosophical capacity and technique offered him,
from 1797, new speculative impulse and confidence while he
clarified his own mystical faith.   There was yet a wider
significance in the friendship of these two poets, for they
were to change the course of English poetry with an historic
influence that is alive to-day.   The two men were at one in
their sympathies and interests, but they differed widely in
character and in temperament.   Each was a republican, indignant over the war with France ; each had sought refuge
in Godwin ; each was devoted wholeheartedly to poetry and
the things of the mind.   But Wordsworth's mind was tenacious and level, hiding warmth of impulse under northern
reserve ; while Coleridge was by nature volatile, flexible and
unreservedly enthusiastic.[1]   Wordsworth saw that Coleridge
had much to win from his " calmer habits and more steady
voice ;" but Coleridge had, as part of his mind's unquench-
able generosity, a profound sense of tribute to a God of Love,
and his friend, whom he thought " at least semi-atheist,"
was deeply impressed by this religious conception of joy.
By the passionate effusions of Coleridge's *Religious Musings*

---

[1] For instance, when they met, Wordsworth was seeking a quiet home
in an English village ; but Coleridge, with Southey, was projecting a
" Pantisocracy " or Utopia on the banks of the Susquehanna, and he
chose a wife as part of the necessary outfit.

Wordsworth was, to quote Professor Legouis, " wafted beyond the confines of earth." Nevertheless Coleridge had at first the greater gain : schooled in town and immersed in theories, he had missed the contact with those permanent forms of nature in whose images Wordsworth's mind was steeped. Not only did he perceive this fact, but he at once appreciated the added significance with which Wordsworth's genius invested common things. When, in 1798, they launched into the world a new doctrine of poetry, the sincerity that was the keynote of that doctrine was not new to Wordsworth's poetry, for it pervaded the first poem (*The Female Vagrant*) that Wordsworth read to his brother poet. Coleridge saw in it :

> the union of deep feeling with profound thought ; the fine balance of truth in observing, with the imaginative faculty in modifying, the objects observed ; and above all the original gift of spreading the tone, the atmosphere, and with it the depth and height of the ideal world around forms, incidents, and situations, of which, for the common view, custom had bedimmed all the lustre, had dried up the sparkle and the dewdrops.[1]

Coleridge, who was in public estimation far more eloquent and capable than Wordsworth, hastened to tell everybody that his less learned friend was a far greater man, " the latchet of whose shoe I am unworthy to unloose " ; " the best poet of the age " ; " I feel myself a little man by his side." Besides his deep sense of religion and his unlimited enterprise in philosophy, Coleridge offered, then, to Wordsworth the boon of which he was most in need : the faith of a first-class inspired mind in his high poetic genius. Wordsworth accepted that boon with simplicity.

From July 1797 to June 1798 the Wordsworths stayed at Alfoxden, on the Bristol Channel, whither they had moved from Dorsetshire to be nearer to Coleridge. The results of

---

[1] *Biographia Literaria*, chap. iv.

that celebrated companionship are described in a work that
has become a classic of poetic criticism, the *Biographia
Literaria* of Coleridge. It was a spring-tide of poetry. At
the end of that summer (1798) appeared *Lyrical Ballads*, a
little book in which the two young men, not even named on
the title-page, set up an everlasting landmark in English
Literature. It contained the earliest harvest of Wordsworth's
best lyrics.[1] Coleridge's main contribution was *The Ancient
Mariner*. The two poets, working in intimate reciprocity
of encouragement and inspiration, had yet seen clearly the
essential differences in their powers. Says Coleridge:

> it was agreed, that my endeavours should be directed to
> persons and characters supernatural, or at least romantic;
> yet so as to transfer from our inward nature a human interest
> and a semblance of truth sufficient to procure for these
> shadows of imagination that willing suspension of disbelief
> for the moment, which constitutes poetic faith. Mr Words-
> worth, on the other hand, was to propose to himself as his
> object, to give the charm of novelty to things of every day,
> and to excite a feeling analogous to the supernatural, by
> awakening the mind's attention to the lethargy of custom,
> and directing it to the loveliness and the wonders of the
> world before us.[2]

Of the two, Coleridge had the more likelihood of obtaining
that "suspension of disbelief," because his supernatural incidents were cast in an archaic style as "of the elder poets."
No such indulgence was available for Wordsworth. The
public was not prepared to see anything in a ballad but the

---

[1] E.g. *Lines in Early Spring*, *We are Seven*, *Expostulation and Reply*,
It is the first mild day of March, and *Tintern Abbey*.

[2] *Biographia Literaria*, chap. xiv. Hazlitt's remark, from "My First
Acquaintance with Poets," may be quoted here in further illustration of
the difference between the famous pair at Alfoxden: "Coleridge has told
me that he himself liked to compose in walking over uneven ground, or
breaking through the straggling branches of a copse-wood; whereas
Wordsworth always wrote (if he could) walking up and down a straight
gravel walk."

uncultured celebration of some popular story or event ; and
now Wordsworth's ballads put forward lowly themes with a
strange exaltation, and—what was still more perplexing—in
language as bare, apparently, as that of the common street-
ballad. But Wordsworth was making a manifesto. He was
determined to dissociate his work from the affected diction
into which polite poetry had drooped,[1] and he challenged
opinion in a foreword, written and re-written with each succeeding edition of the *Lyrical Ballads*.

Theory of Diction

In his "Advertisement" of 1798 Wordsworth calls his poems
"experiments . . . written chiefly with a view to ascer-
tain how far the language of conversation in the middle and
lower classes of society is adapted to the purposes of poetic
pleasure." In the extensive "Preface" of 1800 he sees that
the justification of poetic utterance is hardly secured unless
urgency of feeling is also demanded by his definition : the
"object . . . was to make the incidents of common life
interesting by tracing in them . . . the primary laws of our
nature : chiefly as far as regards the manner in which we
associate ideas in a state of excitement." [2] The same Preface
includes the remark that "all good poetry is the *spontaneous
overflow of powerful feelings*." In 1802 Wordsworth extends
his statement of diction by proposing to describe incidents
from common life " in a *selection of language really used by
men* ; and, at the same time, to throw over them a certain
colouring of imagination, whereby ordinary things should
be presented to the mind in an unusual way." The last
part of this modification is vague ; but the terms in italics
bear upon the two prime concerns of poetry, namely, What

---

[1] Wordsworth himself had formerly written in this style—see Professor
Legouis' fine examination of the early poems.

[2] The italics in this introduction are not Wordsworth's.

is to be treated? and How is it to be captured on paper? —The themes are to come from compelling emotion and the medium is to be the language of real life, subject to the selection of the poet.

Wordsworth definitely defends the choice of " low and rustic life " as being nearest to elemental human feelings and their uncorrupted expression. The earnestness of the " Preface " is balanced but obdurate, and it led the poet into a position of greater rigour than could be maintained. For instance, the justification of metrical form—that concomitant of urgent feeling—is never really reached. Clearly, Wordsworth takes ample leave to depart from his theoretic rusticity in all his best work.[1] In his worst work he is writing not from compelling emotion but in mere illustration of his theories or poetic manifesto. The result is then plainly pedestrian, and admission of that fact, with the reason of it, could have saved much breath wasted in derision of Wordsworth.[2] Even when his work is bleak and dull, passages occur that take one unawares with their lucent penetration ; and there is ample poetry of lyrical impulse and of sustained exaltation outweighing by far the importance of the ballads. It is upon this opinion that the choice of poems in the present volume is made.

Wordsworth had now provoked opposition and was for a moment appalled by it. The " Preface," however, had brought out his mettle, and he was not likely to look back from the confidence that had framed such sentences as :

> I have at all times endeavoured to look steadily at my subject ;

---

[1] See the celebrated passages in *Biographia Literaria*.

[2] Wordsworth makes an admission on the subject, both modest and proud : . . . " sometimes from diseased impulses I may have written on unworthy subjects. . . . But it is dangerous to make these alterations on the simple authority of a few individuals. . . ."—*Preface* to *Lyrical Ballads*.

Poetry is the breath and finer spirit of all knowledge ; it is the impassioned impression which is the countenance of all Science ;

and the often misquoted

(Poetry) *takes its origin* from emotion recollected in tranquillity.[1]

The murk of stormy times had receded so far as to allow nature's steady images to be recalled, if not with the " appetite " yet with the undiminished strength of youth, and there was now added a deeper insight :

> For I have learned
> To look on nature, not as in the hour
> Of thoughtless youth ; but hearing oftentimes
> The still, sad music of humanity, . . .[2]

When, in 1797, Switzerland suffered from French aggression, Coleridge was stirred to an indignant ode of impeachment,[3] but Wordsworth was already beyond the storm and met that hour with a poem in a very different vein :

> I heard a thousand blended notes,
> While in a grove I sate reclined,
> In that sweet mood when pleasant thoughts
> Bring sad thoughts to the mind.
>
> To her fair works did Nature link
> The human soul that through me ran ;
> And much it grieved my heart to think
> What man has made of man.[4]

Soon the calm grandeur of the poet's native environment, ineffaceable in his memory, was to be restored to him in immediate presence, for, in 1799, after a stay in Germany, the Wordsworths settled in the Lake Country, where, first

---

[1] " Recollected in tranquillity " offers no contradiction to " spontaneous overflow " : recollection brings back the " powerful feelings " in recrudescence.

[2] *Tintern Abbey*, 88-91.   [3] *France : An Ode.*   [4] p. 40.

at Grasmere and then at Rydal, they made their home till the end. The approach of William and Dorothy to Grasmere on foot is described in the fragment " Bleak season was it, turbulent and wild," and there is special significance in the bare words that follow :[1] " the sunbeam said, ' Be happy.' " This was the somewhat naive announcement of an optimism that Wordsworth was now to maintain with characteristic tenacity ; nor was it by any means an optimism of forced growth. The poet's early passion for human liberty was both optimistic and natural. The so-called new diction rested after all on a new heart, one which dwelt on common things and humble people with joy and with reverence, to whose charity nothing was mean. In that spirit *The Prelude* was conceived, and Coleridge now invested the tenet of joy with the authority of his philosophical judgment :

> Joy is the sweet voice, Joy the luminous cloud—

Coleridge perceived, moreover, that Wordsworth's happiness was truly inherent in his character :

> O William ! we receive but what we give,
> And in *our* life alone does Nature live.

Thus Wordsworth in his prime had mastered his griefs, framed his poetic creed, and above all had retained his youthful force. For years there flowed from his mind poetry of an ecstasy governed yet ever fresh, the work of a giant among poets.

Later Life

Wordsworth's period of highest poetic energy lasted from 1797 to 1807. It is undisputed that, after this, the creative vigour which had produced *Tintern Abbey* and the great lyrics declined. In the later work resignation becomes the dominant tone, and the sonnet, once a challenge, becomes a

[1] In the *Recluse* version. *Cf.* also *Tintern Abbey*, ll. 130-134.

solace ; but it is in facing the transition that Wordsworth put forth his greatest majesty and power. There had been premonitions in *The Prelude* :

> I see by glimpses now ; when age comes on,
> May scarcely see at all ; and I would give,
> While yet we may, so far as words can give,
> Substance and life to what I feel. . . .[1]

There is in life no moment more sublime, whether we speak of a state or of an army or of an individual, than that of the determination, when the end is already in view, to put forth one's best with thanksgiving. That sublimity is compassed in the *Intimations of Immortality* with a depth and clearness rarely accorded to man.

The *Ode to Duty* shows Wordsworth's hope that, should the free impulse of nature become too faint to guide us, a sterner, stronger "Power" may yet be our guardian. It had always been his faith that any such Power was the natural culmination of Imagination, whereby humanity merged into divinity ; but he does here seem to call upon a separate spiritual Power :

> I myself commend
> Unto thy guidance from this hour.[2]

The outward events of Wordsworth's life after 1800 are simple. In 1802 he married Mary Hutchinson, already long held in affection by him and his sister. She brought an added

---

[1] *The Prelude*, xii. 281-84.

[2] Wordsworth's sense of some active intervention of spiritual powers has been shown, by the fine scholarship of Professor de Sélincourt's edition (see p. 197), to have inspired an early draft of *The Prelude*, Bk. I. :

> The mind of man is fashioned and built up
> Even as a strain of music : I believe
> That there are Spirits which, when they would form
> A favored being, from his very dawn
> Of infancy do open out the clouds
> As at the touch of lightning, seeking him
> With gentle visitations, quiet Powers !

calm, more placid than Dorothy's, to the Grasmere household. Frugal they were, but hospitable. They still indulged
in feats of walking that surprised, and in Dorothy's case
shocked, their relatives. Family joys and sorrows affected
them deeply. Coleridge was a frequent visitor and, in his
increasing enslavement to drugs, a grave anxiety. The
estrangement between the two poets (1810) was never quite
banished. In 1813 Wordsworth was given a Government
sinecure that placed his family beyond material wants. They
moved to Rydal, where they received from now onwards
visits from distinguished people of letters. It is a pity that
most accounts date from this less interesting half of Wordsworth's life : the false impression, as of a mild pedantic
sage, is thereby strengthened. Wordsworth grew more and
more conservative, and inspiration became more rare. Nevertheless the reader must be careful not to lose the flashes of
vigour that illumined his later years. Dorothy, possibly
partial, says in 1830, " he is still the crack skater on Rydal
Lake " ; and a genial glow can be found in poems written
years after that. Laureate since 1843, Wordsworth died in
1850, peacefully, at Rydal.

III. CHARACTERISTICS

Individual

The foregoing outline will have shown, it is hoped, that the
first characteristic of Wordsworth's mind is its independence.
" I trusted to myself," he writes, " and to the principles of
criticism which I drew from the practice of great poets, and
not from any observations made upon their works by pro-
fessed censors." Or again, " Let the poet first consult his
own heart, as I have done, and leave the rest to posterity."
His independence was apt to harden, particularly in later life,
to egotism. That failing was probably nourished by the limit-

less devotion of the women of his household ; at any rate it was sufficiently marked to tickle the mischievous wit of his friend Charles Lamb : " Wordsworth, the great poet, is coming to town . . . he says he does not see much difficulty in writing like Shakespeare, if he had a mind to try it. It is clear then, nothing is wanting but the mind." But a serious loneliness of spirit was a condition of Wordsworth's power. Coleridge saw it with anxious apprehension : " Doubtless his delights are more deep and sublime ; but he has likewise more hours that prey upon the flesh and blood." Beneath his austerity, however, there is always a profound and touching humility. Thus, *The Prelude* is about his own mind simply because that was the mind he knew best, and the work is, as Professor Garrod says, " mysteriously and divinely void, not only of vanity, but of pride." Crabb Robinson has left an opinion that Wordsworth's praise of his own poems was " never unbecoming . . . but the contrary."

As to sense of humour, it is true that Wordsworth's sometimes deserted him : hence many awkward titles to the poems ; hence also many lines that are favourites in mischievous quotation ;[1] but it is unjust to say that he was devoid of humour.[2]

In the dignity of honesty the poet's work and words abound.[3]

---

[1] For instance, "Spade ! with which Wilkinson hath tilled his lands," —My own choice is :

> On the roof
> Of an itinerant vehicle I sate.
>
> (—Ed.)

[2] See, for instance, the delightful observation of the actor's device at Sadler's Wells (*Prelude*, vii. 286-87) :

> The garb he wears is black as death, the word
> *Invisible* flames forth upon his chest.

[3] Examples are everywhere, but the sincerity with which he restrained the youthful De Quincey will serve to show his peculiar honesty : " My friendship it is not in my power to give. This is a gift which no man can make. A sound and healthy friendship is the growth of time and circumstance."

Wordsworth's honesty does not, however, trail clouds of moral maxims, for he is content to receive his morality from Nature. Even in childhood he feels himself corrected, not by precept, but by the reproach of nature's purity,[1] and to nature is his conscience answerable. [2]

> And I would have my days to be
> Bound each to each in natural piety.

This relation to nature was all in all to Wordsworth, and, difficult as is the consideration of its innermost significance, this much is clear : Nature had endowed him with images so steadfast that he could revert to them, in his time of crisis and despair, for stability against the conjurings of Rationalism ; that he could look to those images still, even when the 'visionary gleam' had departed, to sustain in him the natural piety that was his faith. "Through the fiery trial of the Revolution and Napoleonic tyranny," says Professor Vaughan, "he kept a saner judgment as well as a more heroic temper, than any man in this country." The secret of his level strength lay in his imperturbable relation to Nature : that was what made his character ' homogeneous.'[3]

That Wordsworth's character, once so freedom-loving, became with age so decidedly conservative, is not very perplexing if the reasons are weighed. First, the French Revolution had shaken his faith in democratic wisdom. Second, the country he loved was threatened with invasion. Third, he came to admire some strong conservative friends.[4] Fourth, Industrialism seemed to him to be destroying the dignity of

---

[1] See the "boat" incident, p. 6 ; or the "snares," p. 4.

[2] See *Defrauding Glory*, p. 20, where he has stolen time from Nature for reading.

[3] "I was much pleased with your description of Wordsworth's character as it appeared to you. . . . The word 'homogeneous' gave me great pleasure, as most accurately and happily expressing him."—Coleridge to W. Sotheby (quoted by Harper).

[4] *E.g.*, Sir George Beaumont and Sir Walter Scott.

land and labour and making the people unfit for franchise. Fifth, he loved enduring things. In any case it is not in this period that his importance lies, but in the reaction of his deeply original manhood to the great crisis of his life.

Philosophic

Since Wordsworth had so much of originality and independence of character it will not be supposed that the philosophic beliefs of other men dominated his own mental colour. Like most other people who are not professional philosophers, he was attracted to those conceptions of the nature of thought which seemed most nearly allied to the processes of his own mind.[1] Through Godwin and Coleridge he became interested in the theories of Hartley.

Briefly, Hartley's view was that our higher feelings and faculties are derived from our simple sensations. The impressions of sense are received, they are recognised and contemplated ; and then by habitual association those distinct " vibrations " coalesce into complex conceptions—such as pleasures and pains—the highest being Sympathy and Moral Sense.

As Wordsworth was enwrapt in the message of the senses, as in a kind of divinity, it is easy to see how he was fortified by this doctrine. Wordsworth said Coleridge " compounded a mind out of the senses " ;[2] and Wordsworth declares himself clearly enough in *Tintern Abbey* as

> well pleased to recognise
> In nature and the language of the sense
> The anchor of my purest thoughts, the nurse,
> The guide, the guardian of my heart, and soul
> Of all my moral being.

---

[1] Mr Herbert Read points out that Wordsworth's " Philosophy," like that of Goethe, was " a projection of his personal psychology."

[2] *Table Talk*, 21st July 1832.

The doctrine has a point of contact with an earlier dictum of Locke : " The mind is wholly passive in the reception of all its simple ideas." [1] So also Berkeley : " Sense at first besets and overbears the mind . . . till Intellect begins to dawn." [2] Wordsworth has passages that show similarity of thought too striking to be accidental :

> Nor less I deem that there are Powers
> Which of themselves our minds impress ;
> That we can feed this mind of ours
> In a wise passiveness.[3]

Nature herself provides a lovely image to describe analogously that quiet receptivity of the human mind :

> the visible scene
> Would enter *unawares* into his mind,
> With all its solemn imagery, its rocks,
> Its woods, and that uncertain heaven, received
> Into the bosom of the steady lake.[4]

The Nature that brings such inspiration seems to live and move separately, and to have a will of her own.   Indeed, Wordsworth implies this separate will when he calls a poet a man " delighting to contemplate similar volitions and passions as manifested in the goings-on of the Universe." [5] It is important to notice how far Wordsworth is here from the sentimentalising attitude with which Romantics identified self with Nature.   Wordsworth is usually aware of Nature's independent presence ; opposed to this, he had at times a capacity for brooding within the human soul, until every other form of existence seemed to swoon into unreality.

---

[1] *Essay*, Bk. II., chap. xii. (quoted by Beatty).
[2] *Siris*, Sect. 302 (quoted by Beatty).
[3] *Expostulation and Reply*.   [4] P. 18.
[5] Preface, *Lyrical Ballads*.

Speaking of his childhood, he has a most striking confession of this kind :

> I was often unable to think of external things as having external existence, and I communed with all that I saw as something not apart from, but inherent in, my own immaterial nature.   Many times while going to school have I grasped at a wall or tree to recall myself from this abyss of idealism to the reality.[1]

Lest this should be taken momentarily as an identification, or merging, of Self and Nature, stress should be laid on the word " abyss."   If unity there was to be, it was to come of two distinct elements.

> To her fair works did Nature *link*
> The human soul that through me ran.

Moreover, if the linking is to be undertaken from the human side it will not, for Wordsworth, be achieved by an immediate poetic grappling with Nature.   Nature was not to be caught that way, but accepted in " wise passiveness."   Reverie will be the accumulator of vernal impulse : that store is the best reality and will give the " fountain light of all our day."   The unity with Nature, then, is to have its existence not in immediacy but in Recollection.

> Nor is it I who play the part,
> But a shy spirit in my heart,
> That comes and goes—will sometimes leap
> From hiding-places ten years deep.[2]

Anamnesis, the recollection of first origins, has two applications to Wordsworth's work.   It is often construed as his sense of pre-existence and referred to Plato's doctrine, which will be touched on presently.   Recollection, in the more usual sense, is a main process in Wordsworthian faith and art ; it

[1] Note to Miss Fenwick on the *Intimations of Immortality* Ode.
[2] *The Waggoner*, Canto IV., 209-12.

is constantly in evidence,—for instance in *Daffodils*, in *Tintern Abbey*, and above all in the *Immortality* Ode.   Yet, even in the Ode, the

> joy ! that in our embers
> Is something that doth live

is a joy that harks back not so much to the mysterious shores of pre-existence as to the wealth of illumination gained from the keen senses of youth.

> Sensations sweet,
> Felt in the blood, and felt along the heart.

We have seen how earnest Wordsworth was in this nature-faith : he believed that the pure message of the senses was only to be staled and perverted by the intervention of Reason in the ordinary acceptance of the term.

> Sweet is the lore which nature brings ;
> Our meddling intellect
> Misshapes the beauteous forms of things :—
> We murder to dissect.[1]

Hence Wordsworth's turning, not to a new " diction " but to minds and subjects undisturbed by false secondary reasoning—to peasants, vagrants, children, to half-wits even, and to flowers.   Lamb saw[2] that Wordsworth's object was " to abate the pride of the calculating understanding and to reinstate the *imagination* and the *affections*."

Imagination and the affections : surely, it may be objected, those two are fields of mental energy that are active and

---

[1] *The Tables Turned.*—Wordsworth's extreme statement of this view. Compare *The Prelude*, ii. 216 :

> that *false secondary power*
> By which we multiply distinctions, then
> Deem that our puny boundaries are things
> That we perceive, and not that we have made.

[2] Writing of *The Excursion* in the *Quarterly Review* (quoted by Harper).

complicated, beyond the brooding reverie of the senses, however precious these may be.   But, to the mature Wordsworth,
the senses, which always brought "*visionary* hours," were
precious for the very reason that they, in their unbiassed
purity, were to be the well of life to the higher faculties.
Here Wordsworth doubtless found comfort in the philosophic
authority of Hartley and Coleridge ; but the passionate conviction is his own, in a degree that is unique, and it finds
consummation in his poetry.   The unfolding of the more
complicated emotions will ever remain elusive of scrutiny ;
but Wordsworth gives, more powerfully than any other poet,
their upgrowth from that

> feeling and a love,
> That had no need of a remoter charm,
> By thought supplied.[1]

In *Tintern Abbey* the " beauteous forms " are direct creditors
to the Affections, those " nameless unremembered acts of
kindness and of love."   The deep waters of the senses have
taken a richer if more sombre hue,

> While with an eye made quiet by the power
> Of harmony, and the deep power of joy,
> We see into the life of things.[1]

As for Imagination—that is the expression which, for
Wordsworth, came to mean the grandest power of human
faculty, a power able to combine awareness of nature with

> a sense sublime
> Of something far more deeply interfused.[1]

It is a kind of poised intuition that can combine

> The excellence, pure function, and best power
> Both of the object seen, and eye that sees.[2]

The calculating Reason, that subjects life to custom or

[1] *Tintern Abbey*.   [2] P. 30.

14 C

expediency, ignores our higher faculties, but Imagination is another name for

> clearest insight, amplitude of mind,
> And Reason in her most exalted mood.[1]

In his sense of the creative activity of the Imagination Wordsworth surpasses even Milton's " The mind is its own place," for Imagination becomes for him a Half-Creator.[2] Mind nourished by Nature rises yet higher

> In beauty exalted, as it is itself
> Of quality and fabric more divine.[3]

At this point a word is due upon the Platonic aspect of Wordsworth's " Recollection." Late in life he disdained any definite doctrine of a " prior state of existence " ; but that withdrawal was mainly an elderly avoidance of giving " pain to some good and pious persons." Professor Harper points out that the central theme of the *Immortality* Ode is " the magisterial sanctity of childhood." The *Rainbow*—with the famous line " The Child is father of the Man "—was written about the same time ; and enough has been said to show Wordsworth's trust in the finer impressibility of early years. The speculation as to *whence* the child has this more sensitive awareness is, then, a secondary theme.

Nevertheless, the fifth section of the Ode reopens, as it were, the poem with a striking declaration that is more like doctrine than suggestion :

> Our birth is but a sleep and a forgetting :
> The Soul that rises with us, our life's Star,
>   Hath had elsewhere its setting,
>   And cometh from afar :
>   Not in entire forgetfulness,
>   And not in utter nakedness,
> But trailing clouds of glory do we come
>   From God, who is our home.

---

[1] *The Prelude*, xiv. 191.   [2] *Tintern Abbey*, line 106.
[3] The closing words of *The Prelude*.

Coleridge, to whom Wordsworth probably owed his knowledge of Plato's doctrine,[1] warned us [2] against accepting the
above passage as a belief in ' Platonic pre-existence.' But
Coleridge mistrusts Plato's meaning too. Professor Garrod
carries more conviction in pointing out [3] a fundamental
difference, namely, that Wordsworth's ' clouds of glory '
relate back to gleams of sense-perception, whereas Plato is
a pure intellectualist, desiring always to abstract from the
senses ' the knowledge which we lost at birth.' For Plato
the evidence of a prior state lies in this ' recovery of knowledge,' which leads to the perception of ' absolute truth.'

The later work of Wordsworth draws nearer to Plato, in
so far as it develops a sense of eternal forms. Thus in *The
Excursion* :

> Immutably survive
> For our support the measures and the forms
> Which an abstract intelligence supplies,
> Whose kingdom is, where time and space are not.

The path of approach was different, but the aim of these
two great minds is surely the same. When, in the *Ode*,
Wordsworth speaks of man as

> a Creature
> Moving about in worlds not realised,

when, in *Tintern Abbey*, he dwells upon

> that blessed mood,
> In which the burthen of the mystery,
> In which the heavy and the weary weight
> Of all this unintelligible world,
> Is lightened :

---

[1] *Cf.* also Coleridge's *Sonnet on the birth of a son* (Hartley C.) and
Wordsworth's verses *To H. C., Six Years Old.*
[2] *Biographia Literaria*, chap. xxii.
[3] *Wordsworth*, pp. 115-18.

is he not approaching near to Plato's " What then shall we imagine to be the aspect of the supreme beauty itself, simple, pure, uncontaminated with the intermixture of human flesh and colours, and all other idle and unreal shapes attendant on mortality ? " [1]

" The aim of Plato," says Gilfillan, " was to suggest the thrilling thought, that there are instincts and wants in man which earth and time cannot satisfy, and which, with their silent, uplifted fingers, point to immortality."   " Enough," says Wordsworth,

> if something from our hands have power
> To live, and act, and serve the future hour ;
> And if, as toward the silent tomb we go,
> Through love, through hope, and faith's transcendent dower,
> We feel that we are greater than we know.[2]

IV. CONCLUSION

The influence of Wordsworth is vast beyond the compass of one or of many volumes to describe it adequately.   Upon his contemporaries not only his work but his personality left an immediate impression of greatness.   Coleridge's admiration we have seen.   Hazlitt gives a faithful description [3] including Wordsworth's gauntness, the roll in his walk and the " northern *burr* " of his speech :

> There was a severe, worn pressure of thought about his temples, a fire in his eye (as if he saw something in objects more than the outward appearance), an intense, high, narrow forehead, a Roman nose, cheeks furrowed by strong purpose and feeling, and a convulsive inclination to laughter about the mouth, a good deal at variance with the solemn, stately expression of the rest of his face.

---

[1] *Symposium.*   [2] p. 89.
[3] In " My first Acquaintance with the Poets."

De Quincey in his description [1] says that the countenance of Wordsworth " was certainly the noblest for intellectual effects " he had ever seen. Leigh Hunt had " never beheld eyes that looked so inspired or supernatural. . . . One might imagine Ezekiel or Isaiah to have had such eyes." Haydon, the painter, declares, " I do not know anyone I would be so inclined to worship as a purified being." [2] Crabb Robinson records Wordsworth's entrance into a company differing widely in views, unitarian and orthodox, but " the homage was involuntary." The rationalist, John Stuart Mill, has left glowing testimony to the inward joy and genial breadth he felt in Wordsworth's work and presence. Carlyle saw a " fine rustic simplicity and dignity about him, and a veracious strength looking through him." [3]

Veracity never forsakes Wordsworth, even in his most impassioned poetry ; and it is this watchfulness, akin to that of a man of science, which makes him a Classic among the Romantics. He looked for no escape from reality into pageantry. He did not sentimentalise, nor affect poetic gloom. He claimed no wilful code of morality as the poet's preserve. The abandon of Shelley is as foreign to him as is the rhetoric of Byron. He sought calm as a condition essential to veracity, so that he might report faithfully the passion and the exaltation with which he viewed the world.

It is fallacious to regard Wordsworth as the leader of " The Lake Poets " (there were hardly any) or as the head of a great Romantic School. He was bigger than any School. The only school he ever had was the whole of English Poetry since his day.

For almost a century his direct influence upon his country-men in general was obscured, first by the sanctimony with which timorous people invested his orthodoxy, and secondly,

---

[1] *Literary Reminiscences.*   [2] *Autobiography.*
[3] Quoted by Harper, *Wordsworth*, p. 607.

in his partial eclipse by a succession of poets—Byron, Tennyson and Browning—who made a readier appeal to the public of their generation. In times of stress, however, people have always turned to the strength of Wordsworth, and his influence has spread through other poetry like a slow, strong tide.

In 1879 Matthew Arnold's *Selections* put forth Wordsworth's cause anew, appealing for the freshness of his vision, as against the over-stressed philosophic interest. When England had passed into the struggle of the Great War, many sincere writers felt that the heritage of Wordsworth was the greatest of all gifts to the English in their ordeal. Profoundly, lovingly English, without a trace of pettiness, it was he who had said

> by the Soul
> Only, the Nations shall be great and free.

Midway in those days of darkness and heroism and madness, a young English poet could write of Wordsworth at Grasmere,

> Now over hill and water stays
> A world more intimately wise,
> Built of your dedicated days,
> And seen in your beholding eyes.[1]

An eminent jurist published at the same time a volume upon *The Statesmanship of Wordsworth*.[2] The theme is not surprising when we know that a great Minister for Foreign Affairs, Viscount Grey, has recommended a passage from Wordsworth [3] to be hung up in all rooms where Cabinets meet. Tribute has followed tribute since the war. One of our leading abstract scientists has paid the utmost homage to the truthful capacity with which the poet apprehends things

---

[1] From Mr John Drinkwater's volume, *Olton Pools*, 1916.
[2] Prof. A. V. Dicey, Oxford, 1917.
[3] *The Prelude*, x. 331-34; on ills of foreign intervention.

" at once far off and near " as aspects of the whole spatio-temporal world : " Wordsworth, to the height of genius, expresses the concrete facts of our apprehension, facts which are distorted in the scientific analysis." [1]   And if the thought of Wordsworth could in war reassure a poet of the things that would outlast that din, then we, having seen the disillusionment of war's aftermath, need no less in England to-day the poet who faced facts, but saw beauty.

> He too upon a wintry clime
> Had fallen—on this iron time
> Of doubts, disputes, distractions, fears.
> He found us when the age had bound
> Our souls in its benumbing round :
> He spoke, and loos'd our hearts in tears.
> He laid us as we lay at birth
> On the cool flowery lap of earth ;
> Smiles broke from us and we had ease.
> The hills were round us, and the breeze
> Went o'er the sun-lit fields again :
> Our foreheads felt the wind and rain.
> Our youth return'd : for there was shed
> On spirits that had long been dead,
> Spirits dried up and closely-furl'd,
> The freshness of the early world.[2]

---

[1] Professor A. N. Whitehead, *Lowell Lectures*, 1925.
[2] Arnold, *Memorial Verses*.

SELECTIONS FROM *THE PRELUDE*

Love had he found in huts where poor men lie ;
His daily teachers had been woods and rills,
The silence that is in the starry sky,
The sleep that is among the lonely hills.

Introduction

Oh there is blessing in this gentle breeze,
A visitant that while it fans my cheek
Doth seem half-conscious of the joy it brings
From the green fields, and from yon azure sky.
Whate'er its mission, the soft breeze can come   5
To none more grateful than to me ; escaped
From the vast city, where I long had pined
A discontented sojourner : now free,
Free as a bird to settle where I will.
What dwelling shall receive me ? in what vale   10
Shall be my harbour ? underneath what grove
Shall I take up my home ? and what clear stream
Shall with its murmur lull me into rest ?
The earth is all before me. With a heart
Joyous, nor scared at its own liberty,   15
I look about ; and should the chosen guide
Be nothing better than a wandering cloud,
I cannot miss my way.

(i. 1-18)

Derwent River

That one, the fairest of all rivers, loved
To blend his murmurs with my nurse's song,
And, from his alder shades and rocky falls,
And from his fords and shallows, sent a voice

That flowed along my dreams?   For this, didst thou,   5
O Derwent! winding among grassy holms
Where I was looking on, a babe in arms,
Make ceaseless music that composed my thoughts
To more than infant softness, giving me
Amid the fretful dwellings of mankind   10
A foretaste, a dim earnest, of the calm
That Nature breathes among the hills and groves.

(i. 270-81)

Bathing

OH, many a time have I, a five years' child,
In a small mill-race severed from his stream,
Made one long bathing of a summer's day;
Basked in the sun, and plunged and basked again
Alternate, all a summer's day, or scoured   5
The sandy fields, leaping through flowery groves
Of yellow ragwort; or when rock and hill,
The woods, and distant Skiddaw's lofty height,
Were bronzed with deepest radiance, stood alone
Beneath the sky, as if I had been born   10
On Indian plains, and from my mother's hut
Had run abroad in wantonness, to sport,
A naked savage, in the thunder shower.

Night Snares—and Nemesis

FAIR seed-time had my soul, and I grew up
Fostered alike by beauty and by fear:
Much favoured in my birthplace, and no less
In that belovèd Vale to which erelong

We were transplanted—there were we let loose   5
For sports of wider range.   Ere I had told
Ten birth-days, when among the mountain-slopes
Frost, and the breath of frosty wind, had snapped
The last autumnal crocus, 'twas my joy
With store of springes o'er my shoulder hung   10
To range the open heights where woodcocks run
Among the smooth green turf.   Through half the
     night,
Scudding away from snare to snare, I plied
That anxious visitation ;—moon and stars
Were shining o'er my head.   I was alone,   15
And seemed to be a trouble to the peace
That dwelt among them.   Sometimes it befell
In these night wanderings, that a strong desire
O'erpowered my better reason, and the bird
Which was the captive of another's toil   20
Became my prey ; and when the deed was done
I heard among the solitary hills
Low breathings coming after me, and sounds
Of undistinguishable motion, steps
Almost as silent as the turf they trod.   25

Bird-Nesting

NOR less when spring has warmed the cultured Vale,
Moved we as plunderers where the mother-bird
Had in high places built her lodge ; though mean
Our object and inglorious, yet the end
Was not ignoble.   Oh ! when I have hung   5
Above the raven's nest, by knots of grass
And half-inch fissures in the slippery rock
But ill sustained, and almost (so it seemed)

Suspended by the blast that blew amain,
Shouldering the naked crag, oh, at that time   10
While on the perilous ridge I hung alone,
With what strange utterance did the loud dry wind
Blow through my ear ! the sky seemed not a sky
Of earth—and with what motion moved the clouds !

A Dark Inscrutable Workmanship

DUST as we are, the immortal spirit grows
Like harmony in music ; there is a dark
Inscrutable workmanship that reconciles
Discordant elements, makes them cling together
In one society.   How strange that all   5
The terrors, pains, and early miseries,
Regrets, vexations, lassitudes interfused
Within my mind, should e'er have borne a part,
And that a needful part, in making up
The calm existence that is mine when I   10
Am worthy of myself ! Praise to the end !
Thanks to the means which Nature deigned to
     employ ;
Whether her fearless visitings, or those
That came with soft alarm, like hurtless light
Opening the peaceful clouds ; or she may use   15
Severer interventions, ministry
More palpable, as best might suit her aim.

With Trembling Oars

ONE summer evening (led by her) I found
A little boat tied to a willow tree
Within a rocky cave, its usual home.

Straight I unloosed her chain, and stepping in
Pushed from the shore.   It was an act of stealth   5
And troubled pleasure, nor without the voice
Of mountain-echoes did my boat move on ;
Leaving behind her still, on either side,
Small circles glittering idly in the moon,
Until they melted all into one track   10
Of sparkling light.   But now, like one who rows,
Proud of his skill, to reach a chosen point
With an unswerving line, I fixed my view
Upon the summit of a craggy ridge,
The horizon's utmost boundary ; far above   15
Was nothing but the stars and the grey sky.
She was an elfin pinnace ; lustily
I dipped my oars into the silent lake,
And, as I rose upon the stroke, my boat
Went heaving through the water like a swan ;   20
When, from behind that craggy steep till then
The horizon's bound, a huge peak, black and huge,
As if with voluntary power instinct
Upreared its head.   I struck and struck again,
And growing still in stature the grim shape   25
Towered up between me and the stars, and still,
For so it seemed, with purpose of its own
And measured motion like a living thing,
Strode after me.   With trembling oars I turned,
And through the silent water stole my way   30
Back to the covert of the willow tree ;
There in her mooring-place I left my bark,—
And through the meadows homeward went, in
   grave
And serious mood ; but after I had seen
That spectacle, for many days, my brain   35
Worked with a dim and undetermined sense

Of unknown modes of being ; o'er my thoughts
There hung a darkness, call it solitude
Or blank desertion.   No familiar shapes
Remained, no pleasant images of trees,   40
Of sea or sky, no colours of green fields ;
But huge and mighty forms that do not live,
Like living men, moved slowly through the mind
By day, and were a trouble to my dreams.

Nature's Dower

WISDOM and Spirit of the universe !
Thou Soul that art the eternity of thought,
That givest to forms and images a breath
And everlasting motion, not in vain
By day or star-light thus from my first dawn   5
Of childhood didst thou intertwine for me
The passions that build up our human soul ;
Not with the mean and vulgar works of man,
But with high objects, with enduring things—
With life and nature—purifying thus   10
The elements of feeling and of thought,
And sanctifying, by such discipline,
Both pain and fear, until we recognise
A grandeur in the beatings of the heart.

School Days at Hawkshead rich in Seasonable Joys

NOR was this fellowship vouchsafed to me
With stinted kindness.   In November days,
When vapours rolling down the valley made
A lonely scene more lonesome, among woods,

At noon and 'mid the calm of summer nights, 5
When, by the margin of the trembling lake,
Beneath the gloomy hills homeward I went
In solitude, such intercourse was mine ;
Mine was it in the fields both day and night,
And by the waters, all the summer long. 10

Skating

AND in the frosty season, when the sun
Was set, and visible for many a mile
The cottage windows blazed through twilight gloom,
I heeded not their summons : happy time
It was indeed for all of us—for me 5
It was a time of rapture ! Clear and loud
The village clock tolled six,—I wheeled about,
Proud and exulting like an untired horse
That cares not for his home. All shod with steel,
We hissed along the polished ice in games 10
Confederate, imitative of the chase
And woodland pleasures,—the resounding horn,
The pack loud chiming, and the hunted hare.
So through the darkness and the cold we flew,
And not a voice was idle ; with the din 15
Smitten, the precipices rang aloud ;
The leafless trees and every icy crag
Tinkled like iron ; while far distant hills
Into the tumult sent an alien sound
Of melancholy not unnoticed, while the stars 20
Eastward were sparkling clear, and in the west
The orange sky of evening died away.
Not seldom from the uproar I retired
Into a silent bay, or sportively

14 D

Glanced sideway, leaving the tumultuous throng,   25
To cut across the reflex of a star
That fled, and, flying still before me, gleamed
Upon the glassy plain ; and oftentimes,
When we had given our bodies to the wind,
And all the shadowy banks on either side   30
Came sweeping through the darkness, spinning still
The rapid line of motion, then at once
Have I, reclining back upon my heels,
Stopped short ; yet still the solitary cliffs
Wheeled by me—even as if the earth had rolled   35
With visible motion her diurnal round !
Behind me did they stretch in solemn train,
Feebler and feebler, and I stood and watched
Till all was tranquil as a dreamless sleep.

(i. 288-463)

Other Pastimes

WE were a noisy crew ; the sun in heaven
Beheld not vales more beautiful than ours ;
Nor saw a band in happiness and joy
Richer, or worthier of the ground they trod.
I could record with no reluctant voice   5
The woods of autumn, and their hazel bowers
With milk-white clusters hung ; the rod and line,
True symbol of hope's foolishness, whose strong
And unreproved enchantment led us on
By rocks and pools shut out from every star,   10
All the green summer, to forlorn cascades
Among the windings hid of mountain brooks.
—Unfading recollections ! at this hour
The heart is almost mine with which I felt,
From some hill-top on sunny afternoons,   15

The paper kite high among fleecy clouds
Pull at her rein like an impetuous courser ;
Or, from the meadows sent on gusty days,
Beheld her breast the wind, then suddenly
Dashed headlong, and rejected by the storm.　　　20

(i. 479-98)

　　　　Duly were our games
Prolonged in summer till the day-light failed :
No chair remained before the doors ; the bench
And threshold steps were empty ; fast asleep
The labourer, and the old man who had sate　　　25
A later lingerer ; yet the revelry
Continued and the loud uproar : at last,
When all the ground was dark, and twinkling stars
Edged the black clouds, home and to bed we went,
Feverish with weary joints and beating minds.　　　30

(ii. 9-18)

School-Time Meals and Scanty Purses

Our daily meals were frugal, Sabine fare !
More than we wished we knew the blessing then
Of vigorous hunger—hence corporeal strength
Unsapped by delicate viands ; for, exclude
A little weekly stipend, and we lived　　　5
Through three divisions of the quartered year
In penniless poverty.　But now to school
From the half-yearly holidays returned,
We came with weightier purses, that sufficed
To furnish treats more costly than the Dame　　　10
Of the old grey stone, from her scant board, supplied.
Hence rustic dinners on the cool green ground,
Or in the woods, or by a river's side

Or shady fountain's, while among the leaves
Soft airs were stirring, and the mid-day sun   15
Unfelt shone brightly round us in our joy.

Rides

Nor is my aim neglected if I tell
How sometimes, in the length of those half-years,
We from our funds drew largely ;—proud to curb,
And eager to spur on, the galloping steed ;
And with the courteous inn-keeper, whose stud   5
Supplied our want, we haply might employ
Sly subterfuge, if the adventure's bound
Were distant : some famed temple where of yore
The Druids worshipped, or the antique walls
Of that large abbey, where within the Vale   10
Of Nightshade, to St Mary's honour built,
Stands yet a mouldering pile with fractured arch
Belfry, and images, and living trees ;
A holy scene !—Along the smooth green turf
Our horses grazed.   To more than inland peace,   15
Left by the west wind sweeping overhead
From a tumultuous ocean, trees and towers
In that sequestered valley may be seen,
Both silent and both motionless alike ;
Such the deep shelter that is there, and such   20
The safeguard for repose and quietness.

The Chauntry and the Wren

Our steeds remounted and the summons given,
With whip and spur we through the chauntry flew
In uncouth race, and left the cross-legged knight,

And the stone-abbot, and that single wren
Which one day sang so sweetly in the nave   5
Of the old church, that—though from recent showers
The earth was comfortless, and, touched by faint
Internal breezes, sobbings of the place
And respirations, from the roofless walls
The shuddering ivy dripped large drops—yet still   10
So sweetly 'mid the gloom the invisible bird
Sang to herself, that there I could have made
My dwelling-place, and lived for ever there
To hear such music.   Through the walls we flew
And down the valley, and, a circuit made   15
In wantonness of heart, through rough and smooth
We scampered homewards.   Oh, ye rocks and
      streams,
And that still spirit shed from evening air !
Even in this joyous time I sometimes felt
Your presence, when with slackened step we breathed 20
Along the sides of the steep hills, or when
Lighted by gleams of moonlight from the sea
We beat with thundering hoofs the level sand.

                              (ii. 78-137)

The Palfreys

                        One Christmas time,
On the glad eve of its dear holidays,
Feverish, and tired, and restless, I went forth
Into the fields, impatient for the sight
Of those led palfreys that should bear us home,   5
My brothers and myself.   There rose a crag
That, from the meeting-point of two highways
Ascending, overlooked them both, far stretched ;

Thither, uncertain on which road to fix
My expectation, thither I repaired,　　　　　　　10
Scout-like, and gained the summit ; 'twas a day
Tempestuous, dark, and wild, and on the grass
I sate half-sheltered by a naked wall ;
Upon my right hand couched a single sheep,
Upon my left a blasted hawthorn stood ;　　　　　15
With those companions at my side, I watched,
Straining my eyes intensely, as the mist
Gave intermitting prospect of the copse
And plain beneath.　Ere we to school returned,—
That dreary time,—ere we had been ten days　　20
Sojourners in my father's house, he died,
And I and my three brothers, orphans then,
Followed his body to the grave.　The event,
With all the sorrow that it brought, appeared
A chastisement ; and when I called to mind　　25
That day so lately past, when from the crag
I looked in such anxiety of hope ;
With trite reflections of morality,
Yet in the deepest passion, I bowed low
To God, Who thus corrected my desires ;　　　30
And, afterwards, the wind and sleety rain,
And all the business of the elements,
The single sheep, and the one blasted tree,
And the bleak music from that old stone wall,
The noise of wood and water, and the mist　　35
That on the line of each of those two roads
Advanced in such indisputable shapes ;
All these were kindred spectacles and sounds
To which I oft repaired, and thence would drink,
As at a fountain ; and on winter nights,　　　40
Down to this very time, when storm and rain
Beat on my roof, or, haply, at noon-day,

While in a grove I walk, whose lofty trees,
Laden with summer's thickest foliage, rock
In a strong wind, some working of the spirit,   45
Some inward agitations thence are brought,
Whate'er their office, whether to beguile
Thoughts over busy in the course they took,
Or animate an hour of vacant ease.

(xii. 287-335)

Free, as a Boy, to Walk Alone, late and early

            For I would walk alone,
Under the quiet stars, and at that time
Have felt whate'er there is of power in sound
To breathe an elevated mood, by form
Or image unprofaned ; and I would stand,   5
If the night blackened with a coming storm,
Beneath some rock, listening to notes that are
The ghostly language of the ancient earth,
Or make their dim abode in distant winds.
Thence did I drink the visionary power ;   10
And deem not profitless those fleeting moods
Of shadowy exultation.

(ii. 302-13)

Nor seldom did I lift our cottage latch
Far earlier, ere one smoke-wreath had risen
From human dwelling, or the vernal thrush   15
Was audible : and sate among the woods
Alone upon some jutting eminence,
At the first gleam of dawn-light, when the Vale,
Yet slumbering, lay in utter solitude.

(ii. 339-45)

Ye Mountains

YET were I grossly destitute of all
Those human sentiments that make this earth
So dear, if I should fail with grateful voice
To speak of you, ye mountains, and ye lakes
And sounding cataracts, ye mists and winds   5
That dwell among the hills where I was born.
If in my youth I have been pure in heart,
If, mingling with the world, I am content
With my own modest pleasures, and have lived
With God and Nature communing, removed   10
From little enmities and low desires,
The gift is yours.

(ii. 421-32)

[Wordsworth now goes to Cambridge, but the influence of
Nature, gathered from his beloved Vale, remains stronger than
that of academic pursuits. The following passage refers to the
cottage and bed at Hawkshead whither he returns for his first
vacation.]

That lowly bed whence I had heard the wind
Roar, and the rain beat hard ; where I so oft
Had lain awake on summer nights to watch
The moon in splendour couched among the leaves
Of a tall ash, that near our cottage stood ;   5
Had watched her with fixed eyes while to and fro
In the dark summit of the waving tree
She rocked with every impulse of the breeze.

(iv. 85-92)

Gaiety, a Dawn and a Dedication

I had passed

The night in dancing, gaiety, and mirth,
With din of instruments and shuffling feet,
And glancing forms, and tapers glittering,
And unaimed prattle flying up and down ;   5
Spirits upon the stretch, and here and there
Slight shocks of young love-liking interspersed,
Whose transient pleasure mounted to the head,
And tingled through the veins.   Ere we retired,
The cock had crowed, and now the eastern sky   10
Was kindling, not unseen, from humble copse
And open field, through which the pathway wound,
And homeward led my steps.   Magnificent
The morning rose, in memorable pomp,
Glorious as e'er I had beheld—in front,   15
The sea lay laughing at a distance ; near,
The solid mountains shone, bright as the clouds,
Grain-tinctured, drenched in empyrean light ;
And in the meadows and the lower grounds
Was all the sweetness of a common dawn—   20
Dews, vapours, and the melody of birds,
And labourers going forth to till the fields.
Ah ! need I say, dear Friend ! that to the brim
My heart was full ; I made no vows, but vows
Were then made for me ; bond unknown to me   25
Was given, that I should be, else sinning greatly,
A dedicated Spirit.   On I walked
In thankful blessedness, which yet survives.

(iv. 311-38)

Memory of a Kindred Spirit

THERE was a Boy : ye knew him well, ye cliffs
And islands of Winander !—many a time
At evening, when the earliest stars began
To move along the edges of the hills,
Rising or setting, would he stand alone   5
Beneath the trees or by the glimmering lake,
And there, with fingers interwoven, both hands
Pressed closely palm to palm, and to his mouth
Uplifted, he, as through an instrument,
Blew mimic hootings to the silent owls,   10
That they might answer him ; and they would shout
Across the watery vale, and shout again,
Responsive to his call, with quivering peals,
And long halloos and screams, and echoes loud,
Redoubled and redoubled, concourse wild   15
Of jocund din ; and, when a lengthened pause
Of silence came and baffled his best skill,
Then sometimes, in that silence while he hung
Listening, a gentle shock of mild surprise
Has carried far into his heart the voice   20
Of mountain torrents ; or the visible scene
Would enter unawares into his mind,
With all its solemn imagery, its rocks,
Its woods, and that uncertain heaven, received
Into the bosom of the steady lake.   25

                              (v. 364-88)

The Drowned Man

WELL do I call to mind the very week
When I was first intrusted to the care
Of that sweet Valley ; when its paths, its shores,
And brooks were like a dream of novelty
To my half-infant thoughts ; that very week,   5
While I was roving up and down alone,
Seeking I knew not what, I chanced to cross
One of those open fields, which, shaped like ears,
Make green peninsulas on Esthwaite's Lake :
Twilight was coming on, yet through the gloom   10
Appeared distinctly on the opposite shore
A heap of garments, as if left by one
Who might have there been bathing.   Long I
    watched,
But no one owned them ; meanwhile the calm lake
Grew dark with all the shadows on its breast,   15
And, now and then, a fish up-leaping snapped
The breathless stillness.   The succeeding day,
Those unclaimed garments telling a plain tale
Drew to the spot an anxious crowd ; some looked
In passive expectation from the shore,   20
While from a boat others hung o'er the deep,
Sounding with grappling irons and long poles.
At last, the dead man, 'mid that beauteous scene
Of trees and hills and water, bolt upright
Rose, with his ghastly face, a spectre shape   25
Of terror ; yet no soul-debasing fear,
Young as I was, a child not nine years old,
Possessed me, for my inner eye had seen
Such sights before, among the shining streams
Of faery land, the forest of romance.   30

Their spirit hallowed the sad spectacle
With decoration of ideal grace ;
A dignity, a smoothness, like the works
Of Grecian art, and purest poesy.

(v. 426 59)

Defrauding Glory

How often in the course
Of those glad respites, though a soft west wind
Ruffled the waters to the angler's wish,
For a whole day together, have I lain
Down by thy side, O Derwent ! murmuring stream,   5
On the hot stones, and in the glaring sun,
And there have read, devouring as I read,
Defrauding the day's glory, desperate !
Till with a sudden bound of smart reproach,
Such as an idler deals with in his shame,   10
I to the sport betook myself again.

(v. 480-90)

Visionary Power

HERE must we pause : this only let me add,
From heart-experience, and in humblest sense
Of modesty, that he, who in his youth
A daily wanderer among woods and fields
With living Nature hath been intimate,   5
Not only in that raw unpractised time
Is stirred to ecstasy, as others are,
By glittering verse ; but further, doth receive,
In measure only dealt out to himself,
Knowledge and increase of enduring joy   10
From the great Nature that exists in works

Of mighty Poets.   Visionary power
Attends the motions of the viewless winds,
Embodied in the mystery of words :
There, darkness makes abode, and all the host   15
Of shadowy things work endless changes,—there,
As in a mansion like their proper home,
Even forms and substances are circumfused
By that transparent veil with light divine,
And, through the turnings intricate of verse,   20
Present themselves as objects recognised,
In flashes, and with glory not their own.

(v. 584-605)

London

RISE up, thou monstrous ant-hill on the plain
Of a too busy world ! Before me flow,
Thou endless stream of men and moving things !
Thy every-day appearance, as it strikes—
With wonder heightened, or sublimed by awe—   5
On strangers, of all ages ; the quick dance
Of colours, lights, and forms ; the deafening din ;
The comers and the goers face to face,
Face after face ; the string of dazzling wares,
Shop after shop, with symbols, blazoned names,   10
And all the tradesman's honours overhead :
Here, fronts of houses, like a title-page
With letters huge inscribed from top to toe ;
Stationed above the door, like guardian saints,
There, allegoric shapes, female or male ;   15
Or physiognomies of real men,
Land-warriors, kings, or admirals of the sea,
Boyle, Shakespeare, Newton, or the attractive head
Of some quack-doctor, famous in his day.

Meanwhile the roar continues, till at length,   20
Escaped as from an enemy, we turn
Abruptly into some sequestered nook,
Still as a sheltered place when winds blow loud !
                              (vii. 149-71)

Two London Pictures

I

A FATHER—for he bore that sacred name—
Him saw I, sitting in an open square,
Upon a corner-stone of that low wall,
Wherein were fixed the iron pales that fenced
A spacious grass-plot ; there, in silence, sate   5
This One Man, with a sickly babe outstretched
Upon his knee, whom he had thither brought
For sunshine, and to breathe the fresher air.
Of those who passed, and me who looked at him,
He took no heed ; but in his brawny arms   10
(The Artificer was to the elbow bare,
And from his work this moment had been stolen)
He held the child, and, bending over it,
As if he were afraid both of the sun
And of the air, which he had come to seek,   15
Eyed the poor babe with love unutterable.
                              (vii. 603-17)

II

Lost

Amid the moving pageant, I was smitten
Abruptly, with the view (a sight not rare)
Of a blind Beggar, who, with upright face,

Stood, propped against a wall, upon his chest   5
Wearing a written paper, to explain
His story, whence he came, and who he was.
Caught by the spectacle my mind turned round
As with the might of waters ; an apt type
This label seemed of the utmost we can know,   10
Both of ourselves and of the universe ;
And, on the shape of that unmoving man,
His steadfast face and sightless eyes, I gazed,
As if admonished from another world.

    Though reared upon the base of outward things,   15
Structures like these the excited spirit mainly
Builds for herself ; scenes different there are,
Full-formed, that take, with small internal help,
Possession of the faculties,—the peace
That comes with night ; the deep solemnity   20
Of nature's intermediate hours of rest,
When the great tide of human life stands still ;
The business of the day to come, unborn,
Of that gone by, locked up, as in the grave ;
The blended calmness of the heavens and earth,   25
Moonlight and stars, and empty streets, and sounds
Unfrequent as in deserts.

                          (vii. 636-62)

Home Country again—and the Shepherd

                Yet, hail to you
Moors, mountains, headlands, and ye hollow vales,
Ye long deep channels for the Atlantic's voice,
Powers of my native region ! Ye that seize
The heart with firmer grasp ! Your snows and
    streams   5

Ungovernable, and your terrifying winds,
That howl so dismally for him who treads
Companionless your awful solitudes !
There, 'tis the shepherd's task the winter long
To wait upon the storms : of their approach   10
Sagacious, into sheltering coves he drives
His flock, and thither from the homestead bears
A toilsome burden up the craggy ways,
And deals it out, their regular nourishment
Strewn on the frozen snow. And when the spring 15
Looks out, and all the pastures dance with lambs,
And when the flock, with warmer weather, climbs
Higher and higher; him his office leads
To watch their goings whatsoever track
The wanderers choose. For this he quits his home 20
At day-spring, and no sooner doth the sun
Begin to strike him with a fire-like heat,
Than he lies down upon some shining rock,
And breakfasts with his dog . . .
       A rambling schoolboy, thus 25
I felt his presence in his own domain,
As of a lord and master, or a power,
Or genius, under Nature, under God,
Presiding ; and severest solitude
Had more commanding looks when he was there. 30
When up the lonely brooks on rainy days
Angling I went, or trod the trackless hills
By mists bewildered, suddenly mine eyes
Have glanced upon him distant a few steps,
In size a giant, stalking through thick fog,   35
His sheep like Greenland bears ; or, as he stepped
Beyond the boundary line of some hill-shadow,
His form hath flashed upon me, glorified
By the deep radiance of the setting sun :

Or him have I descried in distant sky,   40
A solitary object and sublime,
Above all height ! like an aerial cross
Stationed alone upon a spiry rock
Of the Chartreuse, for worship.   Thus was man
Ennobled outwardly before my sight,   45
And thus my heart was early introduced
To an unconscious love and reverence
Of human nature ; hence the human form
To me became an index of delight,
Of grace and honour, power and worthiness.   50
(viii. 215-238 ; 256-281)

In France—Sympathy with the Revolutionaries

    And when we chanced
One day to meet a hunger-bitten girl,
Who crept along fitting her languid gait
Unto a heifer's motion, by a cord
Tied to her arm, and picking thus from the lane   5
Its sustenance, while the girl with pallid hands
Was busy knitting in a heartless mood
Of solitude, and at the sight my friend
In agitation said, " 'Tis against *that*
That we are fighting," I with him believed   10
That a benignant spirit was abroad
Which might not be withstood, that poverty
Abject as this would in a little time
Be found no more, that we should see the earth
Unthwarted in her wish to recompense   15
The meek, the lowly, patient child of toil,
All institutes for ever blotted out

That legalised exclusion, empty pomp
Abolished, sensual state and cruel power,
Whether by edict of the one or few ;   20
And finally, as sum and crown of all,
Should see the people having a strong hand
In framing their own laws ; whence better days
To all mankind.

(ix. 509-32)

Paris—September, 1792

          But that night
I felt most deeply in what world I was,
What ground I trod on, and what air I breathed.
High was my room and lonely, near the roof
Of a large mansion or hotel, a lodge   5
That would have pleased me in more quiet times ;
Nor was it wholly without pleasure then.
With unextinguished taper I kept watch,
Reading at intervals ; the fear gone by
Pressed on me almost like a fear to come.   10
I thought of those September massacres,
Divided from me by one little month,
Saw them and touched : the rest was conjured up
From tragic fictions or true history,
Remembrances and dim admonishments.   15
The horse is taught his manage, and no star
Of wildest course but treads back his own steps ;
For the spent hurricane the air provides
As fierce a successor ; the tide retreats
But to return out of its hiding-place   20
In the great deep ; all things have second birth ;
The earthquake is not satisfied at once ;
And in this way I wrought upon myself,

Until I seemed to hear a voice that cried,
To the whole city, " sleep no more."   The trance   25
Fled with the voice to which it had given birth ;
But vainly comments of a calmer mind
Promised soft peace and sweet forgetfulness.
The place, all hushed and silent as it was,
Appeared unfit for the repose of night,   30
Defenceless as a wood where tigers roam.

(x. 63-93)

Bewildered Offering

YET did I grieve, nor only grieved, but thought
Of opposition and of remedies :
An insignificant stranger and obscure,
And one, moreover, little graced with power
Of eloquence even in my native speech,   5
And all unfit for tumult or intrigue,
Yet would I at this time with willing heart
Have undertaken for a cause so great
Service however dangerous . . .
          In this frame of mind,   10
Dragged by a chain of harsh necessity,
So seemed it,—now I thankfully acknowledge,
Forced by the gracious providence of Heaven,—
To England I returned, else (though assured
That I both was and must be of small weight,   15
No better than a landsman on the deck
Of a ship struggling with a hideous storm)
Doubtless, I should have then made common cause
With some who perished ; haply perished too,
A poor mistaken and bewildered offering,—   20
Should to the breast of Nature have gone back,

With all my resolutions, all my hopes,
A Poet only to myself, to men
Useless and even, beloved Friend ! a soul
To thee unknown !   25

                          (x. 146-54 ; 221-36)

Grief at England's Hostility

   WHEN the proud fleet that bears the red-cross flag
In that unworthy service was prepared
To mingle, I beheld the vessels lie,
A brood of gallant creatures, on the deep ;
I saw them in their rest, a sojourner   5
Through a whole month of calm and glassy days
In that delightful island which protects
Their place of convocation—there I heard,
Each evening, pacing by the still seashore,
A monitory sound that never failed,—   10
The sunset cannon.   While the orb went down
In the tranquillity of nature, came
That voice, ill requiem ! seldom heard by me
Without a spirit overcast by dark
Imaginations, sense of woes to come,   15
Sorrow for human kind, and pain of heart.

                          (x. 315-30)

Disillusionment

                    A strong shock
Was given to old opinions ; all men's minds
Had felt its power, and mine was both let loose,
Let loose and goaded.   After what hath been
Already said of patriotic love,   5

Suffice it here to add, that, somewhat stern
In temperament, withal a happy man,
And therefore bold to look on painful things,
Free likewise of the world, and thence more bold,
I summoned my best skill, and toiled, intent   10
To anatomise the frame of social life.

(xi. 270-80)

But Nature Abides

The morning shines,

Nor heedeth Man's perverseness ; Spring returns,—
I saw the Spring return, and could rejoice,
In common with the children of her love,
Piping on boughs, or sporting on fresh fields,   5
Or boldly seeking pleasure nearer heaven
On wings that navigate cerulean skies.
So neither were complacency, nor peace,
Nor tender yearnings, wanting for my good
Through these distracted times ; in Nature still   10
Glorying, I found a counterpoise in her,
Which, when the spirit of evil reached its height,
Maintained for me a secret happiness.

(xii. 31-43)

O Soul of Nature ! excellent and fair !
That didst rejoice with me, with whom I, too,   15
Rejoiced through early youth, before the winds
And roaring waters, and in lights and shades
That marched and countermarched about the hills
In glorious apparition, Powers on whom
I daily waited, now all eye and now   20
All ear ; but never long without the heart
Employed, and man's unfolding intellect :

O Soul of Nature ! that, by laws divine
Sustained and governed, still dost overflow
With an impassioned life, what feeble ones   25
Walk on this earth ! how feeble have I been.
(xii. 93-105)

Then was the truth received into my heart,
That, under heaviest sorrow earth can bring,
If from the affliction somewhere do not grow
Honour which could not else have been, a faith,   30
An elevation, and a sanctity,
If new strength be not given nor old restored,
The blame is ours, not Nature's.
(x. 464-70)

If We have Eyes to See

NATURE for all conditions wants not power
To consecrate, if we have eyes to see,
The outside of her creatures, and to breathe
Grandeur upon the very humblest face
Of human life. . . .   5
     And I remember well
That in life's every-day appearances
I seemed about this time to gain clear sight
Of a new world—a world, too, that was fit
To be transmitted, and to other eyes   10
Made visible ; as ruled by those fixed laws
Whence spiritual dignity originates,
Which do both give it being and maintain
A balance, an ennobling interchange
Of action from without and from within ;   15
The excellence, pure function, and best power
Both of the object seen, and eye that sees.
(xiii. 283-87 ; 367-78)

Snowdon

The Type of a Majestic Intellect

In one of those excursions (may they ne'er
Fade from remembrance !) through the Northern
    tracts
Of Cambria ranging with a youthful friend,
I left Bethgelert's huts at couching-time,
And westward took my way, to see the sun   5
Rise, from the top of Snowdon.   To the door
Of a rude cottage at the mountain's base
We came, and roused the shepherd who attends
The adventurous stranger's steps, a trusty guide ;
Then, cheered by short refreshment, sallied forth.   10

    It was a close, warm, breezeless summer night,
Wan, dull, and glaring, with a dripping fog
Low-hung and thick that covered all the sky ;
But, undiscouraged, we began to climb
The mountain-side.   The mist soon girt us round,   15
And, after ordinary travellers' talk
With our conductor, pensively we sank
Each into commerce with his private thoughts :
Thus did we breast the ascent, and by myself
Was nothing either seen or heard that checked   20
Those musings or diverted, save that once
The shepherd's lurcher, who, among the crags,
Had to his joy unearthed a hedgehog, teased
His coiled-up prey with barkings turbulent.
This small adventure, for even such it seemed   25
In that wild place and at the dead of night,
Being over and forgotten, on we wound
In silence as before.   With forehead bent

Earthward, as if in opposition set
Against an enemy, I panted up   30
With eager pace, and no less eager thoughts.
Thus might we wear a midnight hour away,
Ascending at loose distance each from each,
And I, as chanced, the foremost of the band ;
When at my feet the ground appeared to brighten,   35
And with a step or two seemed brighter still ;
Nor was time given to ask or learn the cause,
For instantly a light upon the turf
Fell like a flash, and lo ! as I looked up,
The Moon hung naked in a firmament   40
Of azure without cloud, and at my feet
Rested a silent sea of hoary mist.
A hundred hills their dusky backs upheaved
All over this still ocean ; and beyond,
Far, far beyond, the solid vapours stretched,   45
In headlands, tongues, and promontory shapes,
Into the main Atlantic, that appeared
To dwindle, and give up his majesty,
Usurped upon far as the sight could reach.
Not so the ethereal vault ; encroachment none   50
Was there, nor loss ; only the inferior stars
Had disappeared, or shed a fainter light
In the clear presence of the full-orbed Moon,
Who, from her sovereign elevation, gazed
Upon the billowy ocean, as it lay   55
All meek and silent, save that through a rift—
Not distant from the shore whereon we stood,
A fixed, abysmal, gloomy, breathing-place—
Mounted the roar of waters, torrents, streams
Innumerable, roaring with one voice !   60
Heard over earth and sea, and, in that hour,
For so it seemed, felt by the starry heavens.

When into air had partially dissolved
That vision, given to spirits of the night
And three chance human wanderers, in calm thought 65
Reflected, it appeared to me the type
Of a majestic intellect . . .

       The power, which all
Acknowledge when thus moved, which Nature thus
To bodily sense exhibits, is the express 70
Resemblance of that glorious faculty
That higher minds bear with them as their own.
This is the very spirit in which they deal
With the whole compass of the universe. . . .

Such minds are truly from the Deity, 75
For they are Powers ; and hence the highest bliss
That flesh can know is theirs—the consciousness
Of Whom they are, habitually infused
Through every image and through every thought,
And all affections by communion raised 80
From earth to heaven, from human to divine ;
Hence endless occupation for the Soul,
Whether discursive or intuitive ;
Hence cheerfulness for acts of daily life,
Emotions which best foresight need not fear, 85
Most worthy then of trust when most intense.
Hence, amid ills that vex and wrongs that crush
Our hearts—if here the words of Holy Writ
May with fit reverence be applied—that peace
Which passeth understanding, that repose 90
In moral judgments which from this pure source
Must come, or will by man be sought in vain.
      (xiv. 1-67 ; 86-92 ; 112-29)

LYRICAL POEMS

LYRICAL POEMS

My Heart Leaps Up

My heart leaps up when I behold
    A rainbow in the sky :
So was it when my life began ;
So is it now I am a man ;
So be it when I shall grow old,   5
    Or let me die !
The Child is father of the Man ;
And I could wish my days to be
Bound each to each by natural piety.

TO A SKYLARK

ETHEREAL minstrel ! pilgrim of the sky !
Dost thou despise the earth where cares abound ?
Or, while the wings aspire, are heart and eye
Both with thy nest upon the dewy ground ?
Thy nest which thou canst drop into at will,   5
Those quivering wings composed, that music still !

Leave to the nightingale her shady wood ;
A privacy of glorious light is thine ;
Whence thou dost pour upon the world a flood
Of harmony, with instinct more divine ;   10
Type of the wise who soar, but never roam ;
True to the kindred points of Heaven and Home !

THE GREEN LINNET

BENEATH these fruit-tree boughs that shed
Their snow-white blossoms on my head,
With brightest sunshine round me spread
   Of spring's unclouded weather,
In this sequestered nook how sweet   5
To sit upon my orchard-seat !
And birds and flowers once more to greet,
   My last year's friends together.

One have I marked, the happiest guest
In all this covert of the blest :   10
Hail to Thee, far above the rest
   In joy of voice and pinion !
Thou, Linnet ! in thy green array,
Presiding Spirit here to-day,
Dost lead the revels of the May ;   15
   And this is thy dominion.

While birds, and butterflies, and flowers,
Make all one band of paramours,
Thou, ranging up and down the bowers,
   Art sole in thy employment :   20
A Life, a Presence like the Air,
Scattering thy gladness without care,
Too blest with any one to pair ;
   Thyself thy own enjoyment.

Amid yon tuft of hazel trees,   25
That twinkle to the gusty breeze,
Behold him perched in ecstasies,
   Yet seeming still to hover ;

There ! where the flutter of his wings
Upon his back and body flings   30
Shadows and sunny glimmerings,
    That cover him all over.

My dazzled sight he oft deceives,
A Brother of the dancing leaves ;
Then flits, and from the cottage eaves   35
    Pours forth his song in gushes ;
As if by that exulting strain
He mocked and treated with disdain
The voiceless Form he chose to feign,
    While fluttering in the bushes.   40

Impromptu

THE sun has long been set,
    The stars are out by twos and threes,
The little birds are piping yet
    Among the bushes and trees ;
There's a cuckoo, and one or two thrushes,   5
And a far-off wind that rushes,
And a sound of water that gushes,
And the cuckoo's sovereign cry
Fills all the hollow of the sky.

LINES WRITTEN IN EARLY SPRING

I HEARD a thousand blended notes,
While in a grove I sate reclined,
In that sweet mood when pleasant thoughts
Bring sad thoughts to the mind.

To her fair works did Nature link   5
The human soul that through me ran ;
And much it grieved my heart to think
What man has made of man.

Through primrose tufts, in that green bower,
The periwinkle trailed its wreaths ;   10
And 'tis my faith that every flower
Enjoys the air it breathes.

The birds around me hopped and played,
Their thoughts I cannot measure :—
But the least motion which they made,   15
It seemed a thrill of pleasure.

The budding twigs spread out their fan,
To catch the breezy air ;
And I must think, do all I can,
That there was pleasure there.   20

If this belief from heaven be sent,
If such be Nature's holy plan,
Have I not reason to lament
What man has made of man ?

TO A SKYLARK

Up with me ! up with me into the clouds !
    For thy song, Lark, is strong ;
Up with me, up with me into the clouds !
      Singing, singing,
With clouds and sky about thee ringing,   5
    Lift me, guide me, till I find
That spot which seems so to thy mind !

I have walked through wildernesses dreary,
And to-day my heart is weary ;
Had I now the wings of a Faery,   10
Up to thee would I fly.
There is madness about thee, and joy divine
In that song of thine ;
Lift me, guide me, high and high
To thy banqueting place in the sky.   15

      Joyous as morning,
Thou art laughing and scorning ;
Thou hast a nest for thy love and thy rest,
And, though little troubled with sloth,
Drunken Lark ! thou wouldst be loth   20
To be such a traveller as I.
Happy, happy Liver,
With a soul as strong as a mountain river
Pouring out praise to the almighty Giver,
Joy and jollity be with us both !   25

Alas ! my journey, rugged and uneven,
Through prickly moors or dusty ways must wind ;
But hearing thee, or others of thy kind,
As full of gladness and as free of heaven,
I, with my fate contented, will plod on,   30
And hope for higher raptures, when life's day is done.

The Withered Leaves

A WHIRL-BLAST from behind the hill
Rushed o'er the wood with startling sound ;
Then—all at once the air was still,
And showers of hailstones pattered round.
Where leafless oaks towered high above,   5
I sat within an undergrove
Of tallest hollies, tall and green ;
A fairer bower was never seen.
From year to year the spacious floor
With withered leaves is covered o'er,   10
And all the year the bower is green.
But see ! where'er the hailstones drop
The withered leaves all skip and hop ;
There's not a breeze—no breath of air—
Yet here, and there, and every where   15
Along the floor, beneath the shade
By those embowering hollies made,
The leaves in myriads jump and spring,
As if with pipes and music rare
Some Robin Good-fellow were there,   20
And all those leaves, in festive glee,
Were dancing to the minstrelsy.

EXPOSTULATION AND REPLY

" Why, William, on that old grey stone,
Thus for the length of half a day,
Why, William, sit you thus alone,
And dream your time away ?

" Where are your books ?—that light bequeathed 5
To Beings else forlorn and blind !
Up ! up ! and drink the spirit breathed
From dead men to their kind.

" You look round on your Mother Earth,
As if she for no purpose bore you ; 10
As if you were her first-born birth,
And none had lived before you ! "

One morning thus, by Esthwaite lake,
When life was sweet, I knew not why,
To me my good friend Matthew spake, 15
And thus I made reply :

" The eye—it cannot choose but see ;
We cannot bid the ear be still ;
Our bodies feel, where'er they be,
Against or with our will. 20

" Nor less I deem that there are Powers
Which of themselves our minds impress ;
That we can feed this mind of ours
In a wise passiveness.

" Think you, 'mid all this mighty sum   25
Of things for ever speaking,
That nothing of itself will come,
But we must still be seeking ?

" —Then ask not wherefore, here, alone,
Conversing as I may,   30
I sit upon this old grey stone,
And dream my time away."

THE TABLES TURNED

AN EVENING SCENE ON THE SAME SUBJECT

Up ! up ! my Friend, and quit your books ;
Or surely you'll grow double :
Up ! up ! my Friend, and clear your looks ;
Why all this toil and trouble ?

The sun, above the mountain's head,   5
A freshening lustre mellow
Through all the long green fields has spread,
His first sweet evening yellow.

Books ! 'tis a dull and endless strife :
Come, hear the woodland linnet,   10
How sweet his music ! on my life,
There's more of wisdom in it.

And hark ! how blithe the throstle sings !
He, too, is no mean preacher :
Come forth into the light of things,   15
Let Nature be your Teacher.

She has a world of ready wealth,
Our minds and hearts to bless—
Spontaneous wisdom breathed by health,
Truth breathed by cheerfulness.   20

One impulse from a vernal wood *Spring*
May teach you more of man,
Of moral evil and of good,
Than all the sages can.

Sweet is the lore which Nature brings ;   25
Our meddling intellect
Mis-shapes the beauteous forms of things :—
We murder to dissect.

Enough of Science and of Art ;
Close up those barren leaves ;   30
Come forth, and bring with you a heart
That watches and receives.

THE TWO APRIL MORNINGS

WE walked along, while bright and red
Uprose the morning sun ;
And Matthew stopped, he looked, and said,
" The will of God be done ! "

A village schoolmaster was he,   5
With hair of glittering grey ;
As blithe a man as you could see
On a spring holiday.

And on that morning, through the grass,
And by the steaming rills,　　　　　　　10
We travelled merrily, to pass
A day among the hills.

" Our work," said I, " was well begun,
Then from thy breast what thought,
Beneath so beautiful a sun,　　　　　　15
So sad a sigh has brought ? "

A second time did Matthew stop ;
And fixing still his eye
Upon the eastern mountain-top,
To me he made reply :　　　　　　　　20

" Yon cloud with that long purple cleft
Brings fresh into my mind
A day like this which I have left
Full thirty years behind.

" And just above yon slope of corn　　25
Such colours, and no other,
Were in the sky, that April morn,
Of this the very brother.

" With rod and line I sued the sport
Which that sweet season gave,　　　　30
And, to the churchyard come, stopped short
Beside my daughter's grave.

" Nine summers had she scarcely seen,
The pride of all the vale ;
And then she sang ;—she would have been　35
A very nightingale.

" Six feet in earth my Emma lay ;
And yet I loved her more,
For so it seemed, than till that day
I e'er had loved before. 40

" And, turning from her grave, I met,
Beside the churchyard yew,
A blooming Girl, whose hair was wet
With points of morning dew.

" A basket on her head she bare ; 45
Her brow was smooth and white :
To see a child so very fair,
It was a pure delight !

" No fountain from its rocky cave
E'er tripped with foot so free ; 50
She seemed as happy as a wave
That dances on the sea.

" There came from me a sigh of pain
Which I could ill confine ;
I looked at her, and looked again : 55
And did not wish her mine ! "

Matthew is in his grave, yet now,
Methinks, I see him stand,
As at that moment, with a bough
Of wilding in his hand. 60

THE FOUNTAIN

A CONVERSATION

WE talked with open heart; and tongue
Affectionate and true,
A pair of friends, though I was young,
And Matthew seventy-two.

We lay beneath a spreading oak,   5
Beside a mossy seat ;
And from the turf a fountain broke,
And gurgled at our feet.

" Now, Matthew ! " said I, " let us match
This water's pleasant tune   10
With some old border-song, or catch
That suits a summer's noon ;

" Or of the church-clock and the chimes
Sing here beneath the shade,
That half-mad thing of witty rhymes   15
Which you last April made ! "

In silence Matthew lay, and eyed
The spring beneath the tree ;
And thus the dear old Man replied,
The grey-haired man of glee :   20

" No check, no stay, this Streamlet fears ;
How merrily it goes !
'Twill murmur on a thousand years,
And flow as now it flows.

" And here, on this delightful day, 25
I cannot choose but think
How oft, a vigorous man, I lay
Beside this fountain's brink.

" My eyes are dim with childish tears,
My heart is idly stirred, 30
For the same sound is in my ears
Which in those days I heard.

" Thus fares it still in our decay :
And yet the wiser mind
Mourns less for what age takes away 35
Than what it leaves behind.

" The blackbird amid leafy trees,
The lark above the hill,
Let loose their carols when they please,
Are quiet when they will. 40

" With Nature never do *they* wage
A foolish strife ; they see
A happy youth, and their old age
Is beautiful and free :

" But we are pressed by heavy laws ; 45
And often, glad no more,
We wear a face of joy, because
We have been glad of yore.

" If there be one who need bemoan
His kindred laid in earth, 50
The household hearts that were his own ;
It is the man of mirth.

" My days, my Friend, are almost gone,
My life has been approved,
And many love me ! but by none   55
Am I enough beloved."

" Now both himself and me he wrongs,
The man who thus complains !
I live and sing my idle songs
Upon these happy plains ;   60

" And, Matthew, for thy children dead
I'll be a son to thee ! "
At this he grasped my hand, and said,
" Alas ! that cannot be."

We rose up from the fountain-side ;   65
And down the smooth descent
Of the green sheep-track did we glide ;
And through the wood we went ;

And, ere we came to Leonard's rock,
We sang those witty rhymes   70
About the crazy old church-clock,
And the bewildered chimes.

To the Nightingale

O NIGHTINGALE ! thou surely art
A creature of a " fiery heart " :—
These notes of thine—they pierce and pierce ;
Tumultuous harmony and fierce !
Thou sing'st as if the God of wine   5
Had helped thee to a Valentine ;

A song in mockery and despite
Of shades, and dews, and silent night ;
And steady bliss, and all the loves
Now sleeping in these peaceful groves.　　10

I heard a Stock-dove sing or say
His homely tale, this very day ;
His voice was buried among trees,
Yet to be come-at by the breeze :
He did not cease ; but cooed—and cooed ;　　15
And somewhat pensively he wooed :
He sang of love, with quiet blending,
Slow to begin, and never ending ;
Of serious faith, and inward glee ;
That was the song—the song for me !　　20

I Wandered Lonely as a Cloud

I WANDERED lonely as a cloud
That floats on high o'er vales and hills,
When all at once I saw a crowd,
A host, of golden daffodils ;
Beside the lake, beneath the trees,　　5
Fluttering and dancing in the breeze.

Continuous as the stars that shine
And twinkle on the milky way,
They stretched in never-ending line
Along the margin of a bay :　　10
Ten thousand saw I at a glance,
Tossing their heads in sprightly dance.

The waves beside them danced ; but they
Out-did the sparkling waves in glee :
A poet could not but be gay,   15
In such a jocund company :
I gazed—and gazed—but little thought
What wealth the show to me had brought :

For oft, when on my couch I lie
In vacant or in pensive mood,   20
They flash upon that inward eye
Which is the bliss of solitude ;
And then my heart with pleasure fills,
And dances with the daffodils.

To his Wife

LET other bards of angels sing,
    Bright suns without a spot ;
But thou art no such perfect thing :
    Rejoice that thou art not !

Heed not tho' none should call thee fair ;   5
    So, Mary, let it be
If nought in loveliness compare
    With what thou art to me.

True beauty dwells in deep retreats,
    Whose veil is unremoved   10
Till heart with heart in concord beats,
    And the lover is beloved.

WRITTEN IN MARCH

THE Cock is crowing,
The stream is flowing,
The small birds twitter,
The lake doth glitter,
The green field sleeps in the sun ;   5
The oldest and youngest
Are at work with the strongest ;
The cattle are grazing,
Their heads never raising ;
There are forty feeding like one !   10

Like an army defeated
The snow hath retreated,
And now doth fare ill
On the top of the bare hill ;
The Ploughboy is whooping—anon—anon :   15
There's joy in the mountains ;
There's life in the fountains ;
Small clouds are sailing,
Blue sky prevailing ;
The rain is over and gone !   20

If This Great World

IF this great world of joy and pain
    Revolve in one sure track ;
If freedom, set, will rise again,
    And virtue, flown, come back ;
Woe to the purblind crew who fill   5
    The heart with each day's care ;
Nor gain, from past or future, skill
    To bear, and to forbear !

TO A BUTTERFLY

I'VE watched you now a full half-hour,
Self-poised upon that yellow flower ;
And, little Butterfly ! indeed
I know not if you sleep or feed.
How motionless !—not frozen seas   5
More motionless ! and then
What joy awaits you, when the breeze
Hath found you out among the trees,
And calls you forth again !

This plot of orchard-ground is ours ;   10
My trees they are, my Sister's flowers ;
Here rest your wings when they are weary ;
Here lodge as in a sanctuary !
Come often to us, fear no wrong ;
Sit near us on the bough !   15
We'll talk of sunshine and of song,
And summer days, when we were young ;
Sweet childish days, that were as long
As twenty days are now.

TO MY SISTER

IT is the first mild day of March :
Each minute sweeter than before,
The redbreast sings from the tall larch
That stands beside our door.

There is a blessing in the air,   5
Which seems a sense of joy to yield
To the bare trees, and mountains bare,
And grass in the green field.

(Excerpt)

TO THE CUCKOO

O BLITHE New-comer ! I have heard,
I hear thee and rejoice.
O Cuckoo ! shall I call thee Bird,
Or but a wandering Voice ?

While I am lying on the grass   5
Thy twofold shout I hear ;
From hill to hill it seems to pass
At once far off, and near.

Though babbling only to the Vale,
Of sunshine and of flowers,   10
Thou bringest unto me a tale
Of visionary hours.

Thrice welcome, darling of the Spring !
Even yet thou art to me
No bird, but an invisible thing,   15
A voice, a mystery ;

The same whom in my schoolboy days
I listened to ; that Cry
Which made me look a thousand ways
In bush, and tree, and sky.   20

To seek thee did I often rove
Through woods and on the green ;
And thou wert still a hope, a love ;
Still longed for, never seen.

And I can listen to thee yet ;   25
Can lie upon the plain
And listen, till I do beget
That golden time again.

O blessèd Bird ! the earth we pace
Again appears to be   30
An unsubstantial, faery place ;
That is fit home for Thee !

THE REVERIE OF POOR SUSAN

AT the corner of Wood Street, when daylight appears,
Hangs a Thrush that sings loud, it has sung for three
    years :
Poor Susan has passed by the spot, and has heard
In the silence of morning the song of the Bird.

'Tis a note of enchantment ; what ails her ? She sees   5
A mountain ascending, a vision of trees ;
Bright volumes of vapour through Lothbury glide,
And a river flows on through the vale of Cheapside.

Green pastures she views in the midst of the dale,
Down which she so often has tripped with her pail ;   10
And a single small cottage, a nest like a dove's,
The one only dwelling on earth that she loves.

She looks, and her heart is in heaven : but they fade,
The mist and the river, the hill and the shade :
The stream will not flow, and the hill will not rise,   15
And the colours have all passed away from her eyes !

THE SOLITARY REAPER

BEHOLD her, single in the field,
Yon solitary Highland Lass !
Reaping and singing by herself ;
Stop here, or gently pass !
Alone she cuts and binds the grain, 5
And sings a melancholy strain ;
O listen ! for the Vale profound
Is overflowing with the sound.

No Nightingale did ever chaunt
More welcome notes to weary bands 10
Of travellers in some shady haunt,
Among Arabian sands :
A voice so thrilling ne'er was heard
In spring-time from the Cuckoo-bird,
Breaking the silence of the seas 15
Among the farthest Hebrides.

Will no one tell me what she sings ?—
Perhaps the plaintive numbers flow
For old, unhappy, far-off things,
And battles long ago : 20
Or is it some more humble lay,
Familiar matter of to-day ?
Some natural sorrow, loss, or pain,
That has been, and may be again ?

Whate'er the theme, the Maiden sang 25
As if her song could have no ending ;
I saw her singing at her work,
And o'er the sickle bending ;—

14 G

I listened, motionless and still ;
And, as I mounted up the hill,   30
The music in my heart I bore,
Long after it was heard no more.

AT THE GRAVE OF BURNS
1803

SEVEN YEARS AFTER HIS DEATH

I SHIVER, Spirit fierce and bold,
At thought of what I now behold :
As vapours breathed from dungeons cold
　　　Strike pleasure dead,
So sadness comes from out the mould   5
　　　Where Burns is laid.

And have I then thy bones so near,
And thou forbidden to appear ?
As if it were thyself that's here
　　　I shrink with pain ;   10
And both my wishes and my fear
　　　Alike are vain.

Off weight—nor press on weight !—away
Dark thoughts !—they came, but not to stay ;
With chastened feelings would I pay   15
　　　The tribute due
To him, and aught that hides his clay
　　　From mortal view.

Fresh as the flower, whose modest worth
He sang, his genius " glinted " forth,   20

Rose like a star that touching earth,
    For so it seems,
Doth glorify its humble birth
    With matchless beams.

The piercing eye, the thoughtful brow,   25
The struggling heart, where be they now ?—
Full soon the Aspirant of the plough,
    The prompt, the brave,
Slept, with the obscurest, in the low
    And silent grave.   30

I mourned with thousands, but as one
More deeply grieved, for He was gone
Whose light I hailed when first it shone,
    And showed my youth
How Verse may build a princely throne   35
    On humble truth.

Alas ! where'er the current tends,
Regret pursues and with it blends,—
Huge Criffel's hoary top ascends
    By Skiddaw seen,—   40
Neighbours we were, and loving friends
    We might have been ;

True friends though diversely inclined ;
But heart with heart and mind with mind,
Where the main fibres are entwined,   45
    Through Nature's skill,
May even by contraries be joined
    More closely still.

The tear will start, and let it flow ;
Thou " poor Inhabitant below,"   50
At this dread moment—even so—
  Might we together
Have sate and talked where gowans blow,
  Or on wild heather.

What treasures would have then been placed   55
Within my reach ; of knowledge graced
By fancy what a rich repast !
  But why go on ?—
Oh ! spare to sweep, thou mournful blast,
  His grave grass-grown.   60

There, too, a Son, his joy and pride,
(Not three weeks past the Stripling died,)
Lies gathered to his Father's side,
  Soul-moving sight !
Yet one to which is not denied   65
  Some sad delight.

For *he* is safe, a quiet bed
Hath early found among the dead,
Harboured where none can be misled,
  Wronged, or distrest ;   70
And surely here it may be said
  That such are blest.

And oh for Thee, by pitying grace
Checked oft-times in a devious race,
May He, who halloweth the place   75
  Where Man is laid,
Receive thy Spirit in the embrace
  For which it prayed !

Sighing I turned away ; but ere
Night fell I heard, or seemed to hear,   80
Music that sorrow comes not near,
    A ritual hymn,
Chanted in love that casts out fear
    By Seraphim.

STEPPING WESTWARD

While my Fellow-traveller and I were walking by the side of Loch Ketterine, one fine evening after sunset, in our road to a Hut where, in the course of our Tour, we had been hospitably entertained some weeks before, we met, in one of the loneliest parts of that solitary region, two well-dressed Women, one of whom said to us, by way of greeting, " What, you are stepping westward ? "

" *WHAT, you are stepping westward !* "—" *Yea.*"
—'Twould be a *wildish* destiny,
If we, who thus together roam
In a strange Land, and far from home,
Were in this place the guests of Chance :   5
Yet who would stop, or fear to advance,
Though home or shelter he had none,
With such a sky to lead him on ?

The dewy ground was dark and cold ;
Behind, all gloomy to behold ;   10
And stepping westward seemed to be
A kind of *heavenly* destiny :
I liked the greeting ; 'twas a sound
Of something without place or bound ;
And seemed to give me spiritual right   15
To travel through that region bright.

The voice was soft, and she who spake
Was walking by her native lake :
The salutation had to me
The very sound of courtesy :   20
Its power was felt ; and while my eye
Was fixed upon the glowing Sky,
The echo of the voice enwrought
A human sweetness with the thought
Of travelling through the world that lay   25
Before me in my endless way.

LINES

Composed at Grasmere, during a walk one Evening, after a stormy day, the Author having just read in a Newspaper that the dissolution of Mr Fox was hourly expected.

Loud is the Vale ! the Voice is up
With which she speaks when storms are gone,
A mighty unison of streams !
Of all her Voices, One !

Loud is the Vale ;—this inland Depth   5
In peace is roaring like the Sea ;
Yon star upon the mountain-top
Is listening quietly.

Sad was I, even to pain deprest,
Importunate and heavy load !   10
The Comforter hath found me here,
Upon this lonely road ;

And many thousands now are sad—
Wait the fulfilment of their fear ;
For he must die who is their stay,   15
Their glory disappear.

A Power is passing from the earth
To breathless Nature's dark abyss ;
But when the great and good depart
What is it more than this—   20

That Man, who is from God sent forth,
Doth yet again to God return ?—
Such ebb and flow must ever be,
Then wherefore should we mourn ?

She was a Phantom of Delight

SHE was a Phantom of delight
When first she gleamed upon my sight ;
A lovely Apparition, sent
To be a moment's ornament ;
Her eyes as stars of Twilight fair ;   5
Like Twilight's, too, her dusky hair :
But all things else about her drawn
From May-time and the cheerful Dawn ;
A dancing Shape, an Image gay,
To haunt, to startle, and way-lay.   10

I saw her upon nearer view,
A Spirit, yet a Woman too !
Her household motions light and free,
And steps of virgin-liberty ;
A countenance in which did meet   15
Sweet records, promises as sweet ;
A Creature not too bright or good
For human nature's daily food ;
For transient sorrows, simple wiles,
Praise, blame, love, kisses, tears, and smiles. 20

And now I see with eye serene
The very pulse of the machine ;
A Being breathing thoughtful breath,
A Traveller between life and death ;
The reason firm, the temperate will,   25
Endurance, foresight, strength, and skill ;
A perfect Woman, nobly planned,
To warn, to comfort, and command ;
And yet a Spirit still, and bright
With something of angelic light.   30

A COMPLAINT

THERE is a change—and I am poor ;
Your love hath been, nor long ago,
A fountain at my fond heart's door,
Whose only business was to flow ;
And flow it did ; not taking heed   5
Of its own bounty, or my need.

What happy moments did I count !
Blest was I then all bliss above !
Now, for that consecrated fount
Of murmuring, sparkling, living love,   10
What have I ? shall I dare to tell ?
A comfortless and hidden well.

A well of love—it may be deep—
I trust it is,—and never dry :
What matter ? if the waters sleep   15
In silence and obscurity.
—Such change, and at the very door
Of my fond heart, hath made me poor.

THE AFFLICTION OF MARGARET

I

WHERE art thou, my beloved Son,
Where art thou, worse to me than dead ?
Oh find me, prosperous or undone !
Or, if the grave be now thy bed,
Why am I ignorant of the same   5
That I may rest ; and neither blame
Nor sorrow may attend thy name ?

II

Seven years, alas ! to have received
No tidings of an only child ;
To have despaired, have hoped, believed,   10
And been for evermore beguiled ;
Sometimes with thoughts of very bliss !
I catch at them, and then I miss ;
Was ever darkness like to this ?

III

He was among the prime in worth,   15
An object beauteous to behold ;
Well born, well bred ; I sent him forth
Ingenuous, innocent, and bold :
If things ensued that wanted grace,
As hath been said, they were not base ;   20
And never blush was on my face.

IV

Ah ! little doth the young-one dream,
When full of play and childish cares,
What power is in his wildest scream,
Heard by his mother unawares !   25
He knows it not, he cannot guess :
Years to a mother bring distress ;
But do not make her love the less.

V

Neglect me ! no, I suffered long,
From that ill thought ; and, being blind,   30
Said, " Pride shall help me in my wrong :
Kind mother have I been, as kind
As ever breathed " : and that is true ;
I've wet my path with tears like dew,
Weeping for him when no one knew.   35

VI

My Son, if thou be humbled, poor,
Hopeless of honour and of gain,
Oh ! do not dread thy mother's door ;
Think not of me with grief and pain :
I now can see with better eyes ;   40
And worldly grandeur I despise,
And fortune with her gifts and lies.

VII

Alas ! the fowls of heaven have wings,
And blasts of heaven will aid their flight ;
They mount—how short a voyage brings   45
The wanderers back to their delight !
Chains tie us down by land and sea ;
And wishes, vain as mine, may be
All that is left to comfort thee.

VIII

Perhaps some dungeon hears thee groan,   50
Maimed, mangled by inhuman men ;
Or thou upon a desert thrown
Inheritest the lion's den ;
Or hast been summoned to the deep,
Thou, thou and all thy mates, to keep   55
An incommunicable sleep.

IX

I look for ghosts ; but none will force
Their way to me : 'tis falsely said
That there was ever intercourse
Between the living and the dead ;   60
For, surely, then I should have sight
Of him I wait for day and night,
With love and longings infinite.

X

My apprehensions come in crowds ;
I dread the rustling of the grass ;   65
The very shadows of the clouds
Have power to shake me as they pass :
I question things and do not find
One that will answer to my mind ;
And all the world appears unkind.   70

XI

Beyond participation lie
My troubles, and beyond relief :
If any chance to heave a sigh,
They pity me, and not my grief.
Then come to me, my Son, or send   75
Some tidings that my woes may end ;
I have no other earthly friend !

Glad Sight

GLAD sight wherever new with old
Is joined through some dear homeborn tie ;
The life of all that we behold
Depends upon that mystery.
Vain is the glory of the sky,   5
The beauty vain of field and grove,
Unless, while with admiring eye
We gaze, we also learn to love.

Strange Fits of Passion have I known

STRANGE fits of passion have I known :
And I will dare to tell,
But in the Lover's ear alone,
What once to me befell.

When she I loved looked every day   5
Fresh as a rose in June,
I to her cottage bent my way,
Beneath an evening moon.

Upon the moon I fixed my eye,
All over the wide lea ;   10
With quickening pace my horse drew nigh
Those paths so dear to me.

And now we reached the orchard-plot ;
And, as we climbed the hill,
The sinking moon to Lucy's cot   15
Came near, and nearer still.

In one of those sweet dreams I slept,
Kind Nature's gentlest boon !
And all the while my eyes I kept
On the descending moon.   20

My horse moved on ; hoof after hoof
He raised, and never stopped :
When down behind the cottage roof,
At once, the bright moon dropped.

What fond and wayward thoughts will slide   25
Into a Lover's head !
" O mercy ! " to myself I cried,
" If Lucy should be dead ! "

I travelled among Unknown Men

I TRAVELLED among unknown men,
    In lands beyond the sea ;
Nor, England ! did I know till then
    What love I bore to thee.

'Tis past, that melancholy dream !   5
    Nor will I quit thy shore
A second time ; for still I seem
    To love thee more and more.

Among thy mountains did I feel
    The joy of my desire ;   10
And she I cherished turned her wheel
    Beside an English fire.

Thy mornings showed, thy nights concealed,
    The bowers where Lucy played ;
And thine too is the last green field   15
    That Lucy's eyes surveyed.

She Dwelt among the Untrodden Ways

SHE dwelt among the untrodden ways
    Beside the springs of Dove,
A Maid whom there were none to praise
    And very few to love :

A violet by a mossy stone   5
    Half hidden from the eye !
—Fair as a star, when only one
    Is shining in the sky.

She lived unknown, and few could know
    When Lucy ceased to be ;   10
But she is in her grave, and, oh,
    The difference to me !

A Slumber did my Spirit seal

A SLUMBER did my spirit seal ;
    I had no human fears :
She seemed a thing that could not feel
    The touch of earthly years.

No motion has she now, no force ;   5
    She neither hears nor sees ;
Rolled round in earth's diurnal course,
    With rocks, and stones, and trees.

SONNETS

Nuns fret not at their convent's narrow room;
And hermits are contented with their cells;
And students with their pensive citadels;
Maids at the wheel, the weaver at his loom,
Sit blithe and happy; bees that soar for bloom,
High as the highest Peak of Furness-fells,
Will murmur by the hour in foxglove bells:
In truth the prison, unto which we doom
Ourselves, no prison is: and hence for me,
In sundry moods, 'twas pastime to be bound
Within the Sonnet's scanty plot of ground;
Pleased if some Souls (for such there needs must be)
Who have felt the weight of too much liberty,
Should find brief solace there, as I have found.

England, 1802

I

HERE, on our native soil, we breathe once more.
The cock that crows, the smoke that curls, that sound
Of bells ;—those boys who in yon meadow-ground
In white-sleeved shirts are playing ; and the roar
Of the waves breaking on the chalky shore ;—   5
All, all are English.   Oft have I looked round
With joy in Kent's green vales ; but never found
Myself so satisfied in heart before.
Europe is yet in bonds : but let that pass,
Thought for another moment.   Thou art free,   10
My Country ! and 'tis joy enough and pride
For one hour's perfect bliss, to tread the grass
Of England once again, and hear and see,
With such a dear Companion at my side.

II

INLAND, within a hollow vale I stood ;
And saw, while sea was calm and air was clear,
The coast of France—the coast of France how near !
Drawn almost into frightful neighbourhood.
I shrunk ; for verily the barrier flood   5
Was like a lake, or river bright and fair,
A span of waters ; yet what power is there !
What mightiness for evil and for good !
Even so doth God protect us if we be
Virtuous and wise.   Winds blow, and waters roll,   10
Strength to the brave, and Power, and Deity ;
Yet in themselves are nothing !   One decree
Spake laws to *them*, and said that by the soul
Only, the Nations shall be great and free.

III

O FRIEND ! I know not which way I must look
For comfort, being, as I am, opprest,
To think that now our life is only drest
For show ; mean handy-work of craftsman, cook,
Or groom !—We must run glittering like a brook   5
In the open sunshine, or we are unblest :
The wealthiest man among us is the best :
No grandeur now in nature or in book
Delights us.   Rapine, avarice, expense,
This is idolatry ; and these we adore :   10
Plain living and high thinking are no more :
The homely beauty of the good old cause
Is gone ; our peace, our fearful innocence,
And pure religion breathing household laws.

IV

MILTON ! thou shouldst be living at this hour :
England hath need of thee : she is a fen
Of stagnant waters : altar, sword, and pen,
Fireside, the heroic wealth of hall and bower,
Have forfeited their ancient English dower   5
Of inward happiness.   We are selfish men ;
Oh ! raise us up, return to us again ;
And give us manners, virtue, freedom, power.
Thy soul was like a Star, and dwelt apart ;
Thou hadst a voice whose sound was like the sea : 10
Pure as the naked heavens, majestic, free,
So didst thou travel on life's common way,
In cheerful godliness ; and yet thy heart
The lowliest duties on herself did lay.

V

WHEN I have borne in memory what has tamed
Great Nations, how ennobling thoughts depart
When men change swords for ledgers, and desert
The student's bower for gold, some fears unnamed
I had, my Country—am I to be blamed ?   5
Now, when I think of thee, and what thou art,
Verily, in the bottom of my heart,
Of those unfilial fears I am ashamed.
For dearly must we prize thee ; we who find
In thee a bulwark for the cause of men ;   10
And I by my affection was beguiled :
What wonder if a poet now and then,
Among the many movements of his mind,
Felt for thee as a lover or a child !

VI

It is not to be thought of that the Flood
Of British freedom, which, to the open sea
Of the world's praise, from dark antiquity
Hath flowed, "with pomp of waters, unwithstood,"
Roused though it be full often to a mood　　　　　　5
Which spurns the check of salutary bands,
That this most famous Stream in bogs and sands
Should perish ; and to evil and to good
Be lost for ever.　In our halls is hung
Armoury of the invincible Knights of old :　　　　　10
We must be free or die, who speak the tongue
That Shakspeare spake ; the faith and morals hold
Which Milton held.—In every thing we are sprung
Of Earth's first blood, have titles manifold.

NOVEMBER, 1806

Another year !—another deadly blow !
Another mighty Empire overthrown !
And We are left, or shall be left, alone ;
The last that dare to struggle with the Foe.
'Tis well ! from this day forward we shall know　　　5
That in ourselves our safety must be sought ;
That by our own right hands it must be wrought ;
That we must stand unpropped, or be laid low.
O dastard whom such foretaste doth not cheer !
We shall exult, if they who rule the land　　　　　10
Be men who hold its many blessings dear,
Wise, upright, valiant ; not a servile band,
Who are to judge of danger which they fear,
And honour which they do not understand.

COMPOSED UPON WESTMINSTER BRIDGE, SEPTEMBER 3, 1802

EARTH has not anything to show more fair :
Dull would he be of soul who could pass by
A sight so touching in its majesty :
This City now doth, like a garment, wear
The beauty of the morning ; silent, bare,   5
Ships, towers, domes, theatres, and temples lie
Open unto the fields, and to the sky ;
All bright and glittering in the smokeless air.
Never did sun more beautifully steep
In his first splendour, valley, rock, or hill ;   10
Ne'er saw I, never felt, a calm so deep !
The river glideth at his own sweet will :
Dear God ! the very houses seem asleep ;
And all that mighty heart is lying still !

INSIDE OF KING'S COLLEGE CHAPEL, CAMBRIDGE

TAX not the royal Saint with vain expense,
With ill-matched aims the Architect who planned—
Albeit labouring for a scanty band
Of white-robed Scholars only—this immense
And glorious Work of fine intelligence !   5
Give all thou canst ; high Heaven rejects the lore
Of nicely-calculated less or more ;
So deemed the man who fashioned for the sense
These lofty pillars, spread that branching roof
Self-poised, and scooped into ten thousand cells,   10
Where light and shade repose, where music dwells
Lingering—and wandering on as loth to die ;
Like thoughts whose very sweetness yieldeth proof
That they were born for immortality.

The World

THE world is too much with us ; late and soon,
Getting and spending, we lay waste our powers :
Little we see in Nature that is ours ;
We have given our hearts away, a sordid boon !
This Sea that bares her bosom to the moon ;   5
The winds that will be howling at all hours,
And are up-gathered now like sleeping flowers ;
For this, for everything, we are out of tune ;
It moves us not.—Great God ! I'd rather be
A Pagan suckled in a creed outworn ;   10
So might I, standing on this pleasant lea,
Have glimpses that would make me less forlorn ;
Have sight of Proteus rising from the sea ;
Or hear old Triton blow his wreathèd horn.

MUTABILITY

FROM low to high doth dissolution climb,
And sink from high to low, along a scale
Of awful notes, whose concord shall not fail ;
A musical but melancholy chime,
Which they can hear who meddle not with crime,   5
Nor avarice, nor over-anxious care.
Truth fails not ; but her outward forms that bear
The longest date do melt like frosty rime,
That in the morning whitened hill and plain
And is no more ; drop like the tower sublime   10
Of yesterday, which royally did wear
His crown of weeds, but could not even sustain
Some casual shout that broke the silent air,
Or the unimaginable touch of Time.

A Godhead

O'ER the wide earth, on mountain and on plain,
Dwells in the affections and the soul of man
A Godhead, like the universal PAN ;
But more exalted, with a brighter train :
And shall his bounty be dispensed in vain,   5
Showered equally on city and on field,
And neither hope nor steadfast promise yield
In these usurping times of fear and pain ?
Such doom awaits us.   Nay, forbid it Heaven !
We know the arduous strife, the eternal laws   10
To which the triumph of all good is given,
High sacrifice, and labour without pause,
Even to the death :—else wherefore should the eye
Of man converse with immortality ?

TO SLEEP

A FLOCK of sheep that leisurely pass by,
One after one ; the sound of rain, and bees
Murmuring ; the fall of rivers, winds and seas,
Smooth fields, white sheets of water, and pure sky ;
I have thought of all by turns, and yet do lie   5
Sleepless ! and soon the small birds' melodies
Must hear, first uttered from my orchard trees ;
And the first cuckoo's melancholy cry.
Even thus last night, and two nights more, I lay
And could not win thee, Sleep ! by any stealth :   10
So do not let me wear to-night away :
Without Thee what is all the morning's wealth ?
Come, blessed barrier between day and day,
Dear mother of fresh thoughts and joyous health !

note onomatopœa
alliteration
assonance
assonance

ON THE EXTINCTION OF THE VENETIAN REPUBLIC

ONCE did She hold the gorgeous east in fee ;
And was the safeguard of the west : the worth
Of Venice did not fall below her birth,
Venice, the eldest Child of Liberty.
She was a maiden City, bright and free ;   5
No guile seduced, no force could violate ;
And, when she took unto herself a Mate,
She must espouse the everlasting Sea.
And what if she had seen those glories fade,
Those titles vanish, and that strength decay ;   10
Yet shall some tribute of regret be paid
When her long life hath reached its final day :
Men are we, and must grieve when even the Shade
Of that which once was great is passed away.

TO TOUSSAINT L'OUVERTURE

TOUSSAINT, the most unhappy man of men !   *a*
Whether the whistling Rustic tend his plough   *b*
Within thy hearing, or thy head be now   *b*
Pillowed in some deep dungeon's earless den ;—   *a*
O miserable Chieftain ! where and when   *a*   5
Wilt thou find patience ! Yet die not ; do thou   *b*
Wear rather in thy bonds a cheerful brow :   *b*
Though fallen thyself, never to rise again,   *a*
Live, and take comfort. Thou hast left behind   *c*
name Powers that will work for thee ; air, earth, and skies ; *d* 10
There's not a breathing of the common wind   *c*
That will forget thee ; thou hast great allies ;   *d*
Thy friends are exultations, agonies,   *d*
And love, and man's unconquerable mind.   *c*

MARY QUEEN OF SCOTS

LANDING AT THE MOUTH OF THE DERWENT, WORKINGTON

DEAR to the Loves, and to the Graces vowed,
The Queen drew back the wimple that she wore ;
And to the throng, that on the Cumbrian shore
Her landing hailed, how touchingly she bowed !
And like a Star (that, from a heavy cloud   5
Of pine-tree foliage poised in air, forth darts,
When a soft summer gale at evening parts
The gloom that did its loveliness enshroud)
She smiled ; but Time, the old Saturnian seer,
Sighed on the wing as her foot pressed the strand,   10
With step prelusive to a long array
Of woes and degradations hand in hand—
Weeping captivity, and shuddering fear
Stilled by the ensanguined block of Fotheringay !

TO LADY FITZGERALD, IN HER SEVENTIETH YEAR

SUCH age how beautiful ! O Lady bright,
Whose mortal lineaments seem all refined
By favouring Nature and a saintly Mind
To something purer and more exquisite
Than flesh and blood; whene'er thou meet'st my sight,   5
When I behold thy blanched unwithered cheek,
Thy temples fringed with locks of gleaming white,
And head that droops because the soul is meek,
Thee with the welcome Snowdrop I compare ;
That child of winter, prompting thoughts that climb   10
From desolation toward the genial prime ;
Or with the Moon conquering earth's misty air,
And filling more and more with crystal light
As pensive Evening deepens into night.

PERSONAL TALK

I

I AM not One who much or oft delight
To season my fireside with personal talk,—
Of friends, who live within an easy walk,
Or neighbours, daily, weekly, in my sight :
And, for my chance-acquaintance, ladies bright,   5
Sons, mothers, maidens withering on the stalk,
These all wear out of me, like Forms with chalk
Painted on rich men's floors, for one feast-night.
Better than such discourse doth silence long,
Long, barren silence, square with my desire ;   10
To sit without emotion, hope, or aim,
In the loved presence of my cottage-fire,
And listen to the flapping of the flame,
Or kettle whispering its faint under-song.

II

WINGS have we,—and as far as we can go
We may find pleasure : wilderness and wood,
Blank ocean and mere sky, support that mood
Which with the lofty sanctifies the low.
Dreams, books, are each a world; and books, we know,   5
Are a substantial world, both pure and good :
Round these, with tendrils strong as flesh and blood,
Our pastime and our happiness will grow.
There find I personal themes, a plenteous store,
Matter wherein right voluble I am,   10
To which I listen with a ready ear ;
Two shall be named, pre-eminently dear,—
The gentle Lady married to the Moor ;
And heavenly Una with her milk-white Lamb.

III

Nor can I not believe but that hereby
Great gains are mine ; for thus I live remote
From evil-speaking ; rancour, never sought, *spite.*
Comes to me not ; malignant truth, or lie.
Hence have I genial seasons, hence have I   5
Smooth passions, smooth discourse, and joyous thought :
And thus from day to day my little boat
Rocks in its harbour, lodging peaceably.
Blessings be with them—and eternal praise,
Who gave us nobler loves, and nobler cares—   10
The Poets, who on earth have made us heirs
Of truth and pure delight by heavenly lays !
Oh ! might my name be numbered among theirs,
Then gladly would I end my mortal days.

Twilight

Hail, Twilight, sovereign of one peaceful hour !
Not dull art Thou as undiscerning Night ;
But studious only to remove from sight
Day's mutable distinctions.—Ancient Power !
Thus did the waters gleam, the mountains lower,   5
To the rude Briton, when, in wolf-skin vest
Here roving wild, he laid him down to rest
On the bare rock, or through a leafy bower
Looked ere his eyes were closed. By him was seen
The self-same Vision which we now behold,   10
At thy meek bidding, shadowy Power! brought forth;
These mighty barriers, and the gulf between ;
The flood, the stars,—a spectacle as old
As the beginning of the heavens and earth !

It is a Beauteous Evening

IT is a beauteous evening, calm and free,
The holy time is quiet as a Nun   *a spiritual beauty*
Breathless with adoration ; the broad sun   *(quiet*
Is sinking down in its tranquillity ;
The gentleness of heaven broods o'er the Sea :   5
Listen ! the mighty Being is awake,
And doth with his eternal motion make
A sound like thunder—everlastingly.
Dear Child ! dear Girl ! that walkest with me here,
If thou appear untouched by solemn thought,   10
Thy nature is not therefore less divine :
Thou liest in Abraham's bosom all the year ;
And worshipp'st at the Temple's inner shrine,
God being with thee when we know it not.

Speak !

WHY art thou silent !   Is thy love a plant
Of such weak fibre that the treacherous air
Of absence withers what was once so fair ?
Is there no debt to pay, no boon to grant ?
Yet have my thoughts for thee been vigilant—   5
Bound to thy service with unceasing care,
The mind's least generous wish a mendicant   *beggar*
For nought but what thy happiness could spare.
Speak—though this soft warm heart, once free to hold
A thousand tender pleasures, thine and mine,   10
Be left more desolate, more dreary cold
Than a forsaken bird's-nest filled with snow
'Mid its own bush of leafless eglantine—
Speak, that my torturing doubts their end may know !

Most Grievous Loss

SURPRISED by joy—impatient as the Wind
I turned to share the transport—Oh ! with whom *delight*
But Thee, deep buried in the silent tomb,
That spot which no vicissitude can find ? *change of feeling . emotion.*
Love, faithful love, recalled thee to my mind—   5
But how could I forget thee ?   Through what power,
Even for the least division of an hour,
Have I been so beguiled as to be blind
To my most grievous loss !—That thought's return
Was the worst pang that sorrow ever bore,   10
Save one, one only, when I stood forlorn,
Knowing my heart's best treasure was no more ;
That neither present time, nor years unborn
Could to my sight that heavenly face restore.

BETWEEN NAMUR AND LIEGE

WHAT lovelier home could gentle Fancy choose ?
Is this the stream, whose cities, heights, and plains,
War's favourite playground, are with crimson stains
Familiar, as the Morn with pearly dews ?
The Morn, that now, along the silver MEUSE,   5
Spreading her peaceful ensigns, calls the swains
To tend their silent boats and ringing wains,
Or strip the bough whose mellow fruit bestrews
The ripening corn beneath it.   As mine eyes
Turn from the fortified and threatening hill,   10
How sweet the prospect of yon watery glade,
With its grey rocks clustering in pensive shade—
That, shaped like old monastic turrets, rise
From the smooth meadow-ground, serene and still !

COMPOSED ON A MAY MORNING, 1838

LIFE with yon Lambs, like day, is just begun,
Yet Nature seems to them a heavenly guide.
Does joy approach? they meet the coming tide;
And sullenness avoid, as now they shun
Pale twilight's lingering glooms,—and in the sun 5
Couch near their dams, with quiet satisfied;
Or gambol—each with his shadow at his side,
Varying its shape wherever he may run.
As they from turf yet hoar with sleepy dew
All turn, and court the shining and the green, 10
Where herbs look up, and opening flowers are seen;
Why to God's goodness cannot We be true,
And so, His gifts and promises between,
Feed to the last on pleasures ever new?

The Moon

WHO but is pleased to watch the moon on high
Travelling where she from time to time enshrouds
Her head, and nothing loth her Majesty
Renounces, till among the scattered clouds
One with its kindling edge declares that soon 5
Will reappear before the uplifted eye
A Form as bright, as beautiful a moon,
To glide in open prospect through clear sky.
Pity that such a promise e'er should prove
False in the issue, that yon seeming space 10
Of sky should be in truth the steadfast face
Of a cloud flat and dense, through which must move
(By transit not unlike man's frequent doom)
The Wanderer lost in more determined gloom.

THE TROSSACHS

beauty spot in Scotland.

THERE'S not a nook within this solemn Pass
But were an apt confessional for One
Taught by his summer spent, his autumn gone,
That Life is but a tale of morning grass
Withered at eve.   From scenes of art which chase   5
That thought away, turn, and with watchful eyes
Feed it 'mid Nature's old felicities,
Rocks, rivers, and smooth lakes more clear than glass
Untouched, unbreathed upon.   Thrice happy quest,
If from a golden perch of aspen spray   10
(October's workmanship to rival May)
The pensive warbler of the ruddy breast
That moral sweeten by a heaven-taught lay,
Lulling the year, with all its cares, to rest !

COMPOSED BY THE SIDE OF GRASMERE LAKE

CLOUDS, lingering yet, extend in solid bars
Through the grey west; and lo! these waters, steeled
By breezeless air to smoothest polish, yield
A vivid repetition of the stars ;
Jove, Venus, and the ruddy crest of Mars   5
Amid his fellows beauteously revealed
At happy distance from earth's groaning field,
Where ruthless mortals wage incessant wars.
Is it a mirror ?—or the nether Sphere
Opening to view the abyss in which she feeds   10
Her own calm fires ?—But list ! a voice is near ;
Great Pan himself low-whispering through the reeds,
" Be thankful, thou ; for, if unholy deeds
Ravage the world, tranquillity is here ! "

SEPTEMBER, 1815

WHILE not a leaf seems faded ; while the fields,
With ripening harvest prodigally fair,
In brightest sunshine bask ; this nipping air,
Sent from some distant clime where Winter wields
His icy scimitar, a foretaste yields   5
Of bitter change, and bids the flowers beware ;
And whispers to the silent birds, " Prepare
Against the threatening foe your trustiest shields."
For me, who under kindlier laws belong
To Nature's tuneful quire, this rustling dry   10
Through leaves yet green, and yon crystalline sky,
Announce a season potent to renew,
'Mid frost and snow, the instinctive joys of song,
And nobler cares than listless summer knew.

JOURNEY RENEWED

I ROSE while yet the cattle, heat-opprest,
Crowded together under rustling trees
Brushed by the current of the water-breeze ;
And for *their* sakes, and love of all that rest,
On Duddon's margin, in the sheltering nest ;   5
For all the startled scaly tribes that slink
Into his coverts, and each fearless link
Of dancing insects forged upon his breast ;
For these, and hopes and recollections worn
Close to the vital seat of human clay ;   10
Glad meetings, tender partings, that upstay
The drooping mind of absence, by vows sworn
In his pure presence near the trysting thorn—
I thanked the Leader of my onward way.

AFTER-THOUGHT

I THOUGHT of Thee, my partner and my guide,
As being past away.—Vain sympathies !
For, backward, Duddon ! as I cast my eyes,
I see what was, and is, and will abide ;
Still glides the Stream, and shall for ever glide ;   5
The Form remains, the Function never dies ;
While we, the brave, the mighty, and the wise,
We Men, who in our morn of youth defied
The elements, must vanish ;—be it so !
Enough, if something from our hands have power   10
To live, and act, and serve the future hour ;
And if, as toward the silent tomb we go,
Through love, through hope, and faith's transcendent
      dower,
We feel that we are greater than we know.

NARRATIVE AND REFLECTIVE POEMS

If thou indeed derive thy light from Heaven,
Then, to the measure of that heaven-born light,
Shine, Poet! in thy place, and be content :—
The stars pre-eminent in magnitude,
And they that from the zenith dart their beams,
(Visible though they be to half the earth,
Though half a sphere be conscious of their brightness)
Are yet of no diviner origin,
No purer essence, than the one that burns,
Like an untended watch-fire, on the ridge
Of some dark mountain ; or than those which seem
Humbly to hang, like twinkling winter lamps,
Among the branches of the leafless trees ;
All are the undying offspring of one Sire :
Then, to the measure of the light vouchsafed,
Shine, Poet! in thy place, and be content.

WE ARE SEVEN

———A SIMPLE Child,
That lightly draws its breath,
And feels its life in every limb,
What should it know of death ?

I met a little cottage Girl :   5
She was eight years old, she said ;
Her hair was thick with many a curl
That clustered round her head.

She had a rustic, woodland air,
And she was wildly clad :   10
Her eyes were fair, and very fair ;
—Her beauty made me glad.

" Sisters and brothers, little maid,
How many may you be ? "
" How many ?   Seven in all," she said,   15
And wondering looked at me.

" And where are they ? I pray you tell."
She answered, " Seven are we ;
And two of us at Conway dwell,
And two are gone to sea.   20

" Two of us in the churchyard lie,
My sister and my brother ;
And, in the churchyard cottage, I
Dwell near them with my mother."

" You say that two at Conway dwell,   25
And two are gone to sea,
Yet ye are seven ! I pray you tell,
Sweet Maid, how this may be."

Then did the little Maid reply,
" Seven boys and girls are we ;   30
Two of us in the churchyard lie,
Beneath the churchyard tree."

" You run about, my little Maid,
Your limbs they are alive ;
If two are in the churchyard laid,   35
Then ye are only five."

" Their graves are green, they may be seen,"
The little Maid replied,
" Twelve steps or more from my mother's door,
And they are side by side.   40

" My stockings there I often knit,
My kerchief there I hem ;
And there upon the ground I sit,
And sing a song to them.

" And often after sunset, Sir,   45
When it is light and fair,
I take my little porringer,
And eat my supper there.

" The first that died was sister Jane ;
In bed she moaning lay,   50
Till God released her of her pain ;
And then she went away.

" So in the churchyard she was laid ;
And, when the grass was dry,
Together round her grave we played,   55
My brother John and I.

" And when the ground was white with snow,
And I could run and slide,
My brother John was forced to go,
And he lies by her side."   60

" How many are you, then," said I,
" If they two are in heaven ? "
Quick was the little Maid's reply,
" O Master ! we are seven."

" But they are dead ; those two are dead !   65
Their spirits are in heaven ! "
'Twas throwing words away ; for still
The little Maid would have her will,
And said, " Nay, we are seven ! "

LUCY GRAY

OR, SOLITUDE

OFT I had heard of Lucy Gray :
And, when I crossed the wild,
I chanced to see at break of day
The solitary child.

No mate, no comrade Lucy knew ;   5
She dwelt on a wide moor,
—The sweetest thing that ever grew
Beside a human door !

You yet may spy the fawn at play,
The hare upon the green ;　　　　　　10
But the sweet face of Lucy Gray
Will never more be seen.

" To-night will be a stormy night—
You to the town must go ;
And take a lantern, Child, to light　　　15
Your mother through the snow."

" That, Father ! will I gladly do :
'Tis scarcely afternoon—
The minster-clock has just struck two,
And yonder is the moon ! "　　　　　20

At this the Father raised his hook,
And snapped a faggot-band ;
He plied his work ;—and Lucy took
The lantern in her hand.

Not blither is the mountain roe :　　　25
With many a wanton stroke
Her feet disperse the powdery snow,
That rises up like smoke.

The storm came on before its time :
She wandered up and down ;　　　　30
And many a hill did Lucy climb :
But never reached the town.

The wretched parents all that night
Went shouting far and wide ;
But there was neither sound nor sight　35
To serve them for a guide.

At day-break on a hill they stood
That overlooked the moor ;
And thence they saw the bridge of wood,
A furlong from their door.   40

They wept—and, turning homeward, cried,
" In heaven we all shall meet " ;
—When in the snow the mother spied
The print of Lucy's feet.

Then downwards from the steep hill's edge   45
They tracked the footmarks small ;
And through the broken hawthorn hedge,
And by the long stone-wall ;

And then an open field they crossed :
The marks were still the same ;   50
They tracked them on, nor ever lost ;
And to the bridge they came.

They followed from the snowy bank
Those footmarks, one by one,
Into the middle of the plank ;   55
And further there were none !

—Yet some maintain that to this day
She is a living child ;
That you may see sweet Lucy Gray
Upon the lonesome wild.   60

O'er rough and smooth she trips along,
And never looks behind ;
And sings a solitary song
That whistles in the wind.

THE SAILOR'S MOTHER

ONE morning (raw it was and wet—
A foggy day in winter time)
A Woman on the road I met,
Not old, though something past her prime :
Majestic in her person, tall and straight ;   5
And like a Roman matron's was her mien and gait.

The ancient spirit is not dead ;
Old times, thought I, are breathing there ;
Proud was I that my country bred
Such strength, a dignity so fair :   10
She begged an alms, like one in poor estate ;
I looked at her again, nor did my pride abate.

When from these lofty thoughts I woke,
" What is it," said I, " that you bear,
Beneath the covert of your Cloak,   15
Protected from this cold damp air ? "
She answered, soon as she the question heard,
" A simple burthen, Sir, a little Singing-bird."

And, thus continuing, she said,
" I had a Son, who many a day   20
Sailed on the seas, but he is dead ;
In Denmark he was cast away :
And I have travelled weary miles to see
If aught which he had owned might still remain for me.

" The bird and cage they both were his :   25
'Twas my Son's bird ; and neat and trim
He kept it : many voyages
The singing-bird had gone with him :
When last he sailed, he left the bird behind ;
From bodings, as might be, that hung upon his mind.   30

" He to a fellow-lodger's care
Had left it, to be watched and fed,
And pipe its song in safety ;—there
I found it when my Son was dead ;
And now, God help me for my little wit ! 35
I bear it with me, Sir ;—he took so much delight in it."

HART-LEAP WELL

THE Knight had ridden down from Wensley Moor
With the slow motion of a summer's cloud,
And now, as he approached a vassal's door,
" Bring forth another horse ! " he cried aloud.

" Another horse ! "—That shout the vassal heard 5
And saddled his best Steed, a comely grey ;
Sir Walter mounted him ; he was the third
Which he had mounted on that glorious day.

Joy sparkled in the prancing courser's eyes ;
The horse and horseman are a happy pair ; 10
But, though Sir Walter like a falcon flies,
There is a doleful silence in the air.

A rout this morning left Sir Walter's Hall,
That as they galloped made the echoes roar ;
But horse and man are vanished, one and all ; 15
Such race, I think, was never seen before.

Sir Walter, restless as a veering wind,
Calls to the few tired dogs that yet remain :
Blanch, Swift, and Music, noblest of their kind,
Follow, and up the weary mountain strain. 20

The Knight hallooed, he cheered and chid them on
With suppliant gestures and upbraidings stern ;
But breath and eyesight fail ; and, one by one,
The dogs are stretched among the mountain fern.

Where is the throng, the tumult of the race ?   25
The bugles that so joyfully were blown ?
—This chase it looks not like an earthly chase ;
Sir Walter and the Hart are left alone.

The poor Hart toils along the mountain-side ;
I will not stop to tell how far he fled,   30
Nor will I mention by what death he died ;
But now the Knight beholds him lying dead.

Dismounting, then, he leaned against a thorn ;
He had no follower, dog, nor man, nor boy :
He neither cracked his whip, nor blew his horn.   35
But gazed upon the spoil with silent joy.

Close to the thorn on which Sir Walter leaned
Stood his dumb partner in this glorious feat ;
Weak as a lamb the hour that it is yeaned ;
And white with foam as if with cleaving sleet.   40

Upon his side the Hart was lying stretched :
His nostril touched a spring beneath a hill,
And with the last deep groan his breath had fetched
The waters of the spring were trembling still.

And now, too happy for repose or rest,   45
(Never had living man such joyful lot !)
Sir Walter walked all round, north, south, and west,
And gazed and gazed upon that darling spot.

And climbing up the hill—(it was at least
Four roods of sheer ascent) Sir Walter found   50
Three several hoof-marks which the hunted Beast
Had left imprinted on the grassy ground.

Sir Walter wiped his face, and cried, " Till now
Such sight was never seen by human eyes :
Three leaps have borne him from this lofty brow   55
Down to the very fountain where he lies.

" I'll build a pleasure-house upon this spot,
And a small arbour, made for rural joy ;
'Twill be the traveller's shed, the pilgrim's cot,
A place of love for damsels that are coy.   60

" A cunning artist will I have to frame
A basin for that fountain in the dell !
And they who do make mention of the same,
From this day forth, shall call it HART-LEAP WELL.

" And, gallant Stag ! to make thy praises known,   65
Another monument shall here be raised ;
Three several pillars, each a rough-hewn stone,
And planted where thy hoofs the turf have grazed.

" And in the summer-time, when days are long,
I will come hither with my Paramour ;   70
And with the dancers and the minstrel's song
We will make merry in that pleasant bower.

" Till the foundations of the mountains fail
My mansion with its arbour shall endure ;—
The joy of them who till the fields of Swale,   75
And them who dwell among the woods of Ure ! "

Then home he went, and left the Hart stone-dead,
With breathless nostrils stretched above the spring.
—Soon did the Knight perform what he had said ;
And far and wide the fame thereof did ring.   80

Ere thrice the Moon into her port had steered,
A cup of stone received the living well ;
Three pillars of rude stone Sir Walter reared,
And built a house of pleasure in the dell.

And, near the fountain, flowers of stature tall   85
With trailing plants and trees were intertwined,—
Which soon composed a little sylvan hall,
A leafy shelter from the sun and wind.

And thither, when the summer days were long,
Sir Walter led his wondering Paramour ;   90
And with the dancers and the minstrel's song
Made merriment within that pleasant bower.

The Knight, Sir Walter, died in course of time,
And his bones lie in his paternal vale.—
But there is matter for a second rhyme,   95
And I to this would add another tale.

PART SECOND

The moving accident is not my trade ;
To freeze the blood I have no ready arts :
'Tis my delight, alone in summer shade,
To pipe a simple song for thinking hearts.   100

As I from Hawes to Richmond did repair,
It chanced that I saw standing in a dell
Three aspens at three corners of a square ;
And one, not four yards distant, near a well.

What this imported I could ill divine :   105
And, pulling now the rein my horse to stop,
I saw three pillars standing in a line,—
The last stone pillar on a dark hill-top.

The trees were grey, with neither arms nor head ;
Half wasted the square mound of tawny green ;   110
So that you just might say, as then I said,
" Here in old time the hand of man hath been."

I looked upon the hill both far and near,
More doleful place did never eye survey ;
It seemed as if the spring-time came not here,   115
And Nature here were willing to decay.

I stood in various thoughts and fancies lost,
When one, who was in shepherd's garb attired,
Came up the hollow :—him did I accost,
And what this place might be I then enquired.   120

The Shepherd stopped, and that same story told
Which in my former rhyme I have rehearsed.
" A jolly place," said he, " in times of old !
But something ails it now : the spot is curst.

" You see these lifeless stumps of aspen wood—   125
Some say that they are beeches, others elms—
These were the bower ; and here a mansion stood,
The finest palace of a hundred realms !

" The arbour does its own condition tell ;
You see the stones, the fountain, and the stream ;　　130
But as to the great Lodge ! you might as well
Hunt half a day for a forgotten dream.

" There's neither dog nor heifer, horse nor sheep,
Will wet his lips within that cup of stone ;
And oftentimes, when all are fast asleep,　　　　　135
This water doth send forth a dolorous groan.

" Some say that here a murder has been done,
And blood cries out for blood : but, for my part,
I've guessed, when I've been sitting in the sun,
That it was all for that unhappy Hart.　　　　　140

" What thoughts must through the creature's brain
　　　have past !
Even from the topmost stone, upon the steep,
Are but three bounds—and look, Sir, at this last—
O Master ! it has been a cruel leap.

" For thirteen hours he ran a desperate race ;　　145
And in my simple mind we cannot tell
What cause the Hart might have to love this place,
And come and make his death-bed near the well.

" Here on the grass perhaps asleep he sank,
Lulled by the fountain in the summer-tide ;　　　150
This water was perhaps the first he drank
When he had wandered from his mother's side.

" In April here beneath the flowering thorn
He heard the birds their morning carols sing ;
And he perhaps, for aught we know, was born　　155
Not half a furlong from that self-same spring.

" Now, here is neither grass nor pleasant shade ;
The sun on drearier hollow never shone ;
So will it be, as I have often said,
Till trees, and stones, and fountain, all are gone." 160

" Grey-headed Shepherd, thou hast spoken well ;
Small difference lies between thy creed and mine :
This Beast not unobserved by Nature fell ;
His death was mourned by sympathy divine.

" The Being that is in the clouds and air, 165
That is in the green leaves among the groves,
Maintains a deep and reverential care
For the unoffending creatures whom he loves.

" The pleasure-house is dust :—behind, before,
This is no common waste, no common gloom ; 170
But Nature, in due course of time, once more
Shall here put on her beauty and her bloom.

" She leaves these objects to a slow decay,
That what we are, and have been, may be known ;
But at the coming of the milder day 175
These monuments shall all be overgrown.

" One lesson, Shepherd, let us two divide,
Taught both by what she shows, and what conceals ;
Never to blend our pleasure or our pride
With sorrow of the meanest thing that feels." 180

RESOLUTION AND INDEPENDENCE

I

THERE was a roaring in the wind all night ;
The rain came heavily and fell in floods ;
But now the sun is rising calm and bright ;
The birds are singing in the distant woods ;
Over his own sweet voice the Stock-dove broods ;   5
The Jay makes answer as the Magpie chatters ;
And all the air is filled with pleasant noise of waters.

II

All things that love the sun are out of doors ;
The sky rejoices in the morning's birth ;
The grass is bright with rain-drops ;—on the moors   10
The hare is running races in her mirth ;
And with her feet she from the plashy earth
Raises a mist ; that, glittering in the sun,
Runs with her all the way, wherever she doth run.

III

I was a Traveller then upon the moor ;   15
I saw the hare that raced about with joy ;
I heard the woods and distant waters roar ;
Or heard them not, as happy as a boy :
The pleasant season did my heart employ :
My old remembrances went from me wholly ;   20
And all the ways of men, so vain and melancholy.

IV

But, as it sometimes chanceth, from the might
Of joy in minds that can no further go,

As high as we have mounted in delight
In our dejection do we sink as low ;   25
To me that morning did it happen so ;
And fears and fancies thick upon me came ;
Dim sadness—and blind thoughts, I knew not, nor
    could name.

V

I heard the sky-lark warbling in the sky ;
And I bethought me of the playful hare :   30
Even such a happy Child of earth am I ;
Even as these blissful creatures do I fare ;
Far from the world I walk, and from all care ;
But there may come another day to me—
Solitude, pain of heart, distress, and poverty.   35

VI

My whole life I have lived in pleasant thought,
As if life's business were a summer mood ;
As if all needful things would come unsought
To genial faith, still rich in genial good ;
But how can He expect that others should   40
Build for him, sow for him, and at his call
Love him, who for himself will take no heed at all ?

VII

I thought of Chatterton, the marvellous Boy,
The sleepless Soul that perished in his pride ;
Of Him who walked in glory and in joy   45
Following his plough, along the mountain-side :
By our own spirits are we deified :
We Poets in our youth begin in gladness ;
But thereof come in the end despondency and madness.

VIII

Now, whether it were by peculiar grace,　　　　　50
A leading from above, a something given,
Yet it befell that, in this lonely place,
When I with these untoward thoughts had striven,
Beside a pool bare to the eye of heaven
I saw a man before me unawares :　　　　　55
The oldest man he seemed that ever wore grey hairs.

IX

As a huge stone is sometimes seen to lie
Couched on the bald top of an eminence ;
Wonder to all who do the same espy,
By what means it could thither come, and whence ;　60
So that it seems a thing endued with sense :
Like a sea-beast crawled forth, that on a shelf
Of rock or sand reposeth, there to sun itself ;

X

Such seemed this Man, not all alive nor dead,
Nor all asleep—in his extreme old age :　　　　　65
His body was bent double, feet and head
Coming together in life's pilgrimage ;
As if some dire constraint of pain, or rage
Of sickness felt by him in times long past,
A more than human weight upon his frame had cast. 70

XI

Himself he propped, limbs, body, and pale face,
Upon a long grey staff of shaven wood :
And, still as I drew near with gentle pace,
Upon the margin of that moorish flood
Motionless as a cloud the old Man stood,　　　　　75

That heareth not the loud winds when they call ;
And moveth all together, if it move at all.

XII

At length, himself unsettling, he the pond
Stirred with his staff, and fixedly did look
Upon the muddy water, which he conned,   80
As if he had been reading in a book :
And now a stranger's privilege I took ;
And, drawing to his side, to him did say,
" This morning gives us promise of a glorious day.'

XIII

A gentle answer did the old Man make,   85
In courteous speech which forth he slowly drew :
And him with further words I thus bespake,
" What occupation do you there pursue ?
This is a lonesome place for one like you."
Ere he replied, a flash of mild surprise   90
Broke from the sable orbs of his yet-vivid eyes.

XIV

His words came feebly, from a feeble chest,
But each in solemn order followed each,
With something of a lofty utterance drest—
Choice word and measured phrase, above the reach   95
Of ordinary men ; a stately speech ;
Such as grave Livers do in Scotland use,
Religious men, who give to God and man their dues.

XV

He told, that to these waters he had come
To gather leeches, being old and poor :   100

Employment hazardous and wearisome !
And he had many hardships to endure :
From pond to pond he roamed, from moor to moor ;
Housing, with God's good help, by choice or chance ;
And in this way he gained an honest maintenance.   105

XVI

The old Man still stood talking by my side ;
But now his voice to me was like a stream
Scarce heard ; nor word from word could I divide ;
And the whole body of the Man did seem
Like one whom I had met with in a dream ;   110
Or like a man from some far region sent,
To give me human strength, by apt admonishment.

XVII

My former thoughts returned : the fear that kills ;
And hope that is unwilling to be fed ;
Cold, pain, and labour, and all fleshly ills ;   115
And mighty Poets in their misery dead.
—Perplexed, and longing to be comforted,
My question eagerly did I renew,
" How is it that you live, and what is it you do ? "

XVIII

He with a smile did then his words repeat ;   120
And said that, gathering leeches, far and wide
He travelled ; stirring thus about his feet
The waters of the pools where they abide.
" Once I could meet with them on every side ;
But they have dwindled long by slow decay ;   125
Yet still I persevere, and find them where I may."

XIX

While he was talking thus, the lonely place,
The old Man's shape, and speech—all troubled me :
In my mind's eye I seemed to see him pace
About the weary moors continually,   130
Wandering about alone and silently.
While I these thoughts within myself pursued,
He, having made a pause, the same discourse renewed.

XX

And soon with this he other matter blended,
Cheerfully uttered, with demeanour kind,   135
But stately in the main ; and, when he ended,
I could have laughed myself to scorn to find
In that decrepit Man so firm a mind.
" God," said I, " be my help and stay secure ;
I'll think of the Leech-gatherer on the lonely moor !"   140

TO THE REV. DR WORDSWORTH

The Minstrels played their Christmas tune
To-night beneath my cottage-eaves ;
While, smitten by a lofty moon,
The encircling laurels, thick with leaves,
Gave back a rich and dazzling sheen,   5
That overpowered their natural green.

Through hill and valley every breeze
Had sunk to rest with folded wings :
Keen was the air, but could not freeze,
Nor check, the music of the strings ;   10
So stout and hardy were the band
That scraped the chords with strenuous hand !

And who but listened ?—till was paid
Respect to every Inmate's claim :
The greeting given, the music played,   15
In honour of each household name,
Duly pronounced with lusty call,
And " Merry Christmas " wished to all !

O Brother ! I revere the choice
That took thee from thy native hills ;   20
And it is given thee to rejoice :
Though public care full often tills
(Heaven only witness of the toil)
A barren and ungrateful soil.

Yet, would that Thou, with me and mine,   25
Hadst heard this never-failing rite ;
And seen on other faces shine
A true revival of the light
Which Nature and these rustic Powers,
In simple childhood, spread through ours !   30

For pleasure hath not ceased to wait
On these expected annual rounds ;
Whether the rich man's sumptuous gate
Call forth the unelaborate sounds,
Or they are offered at the door   35
That guards the lowliest of the poor.

How touching, when, at midnight, sweep
Snow-muffled winds, and all is dark,
To hear—and sink again to sleep !
Or, at an earlier call, to mark,   40
By blazing fire, the still suspense
Of self-complacent innocence ;

The mutual nod,—the grave disguise
Of hearts with gladness brimming o'er ;
And some unbidden tears that rise   45
For names once heard, and heard no more ;
Tears brightened by the serenade
For infant in the cradle laid.

Ah ! not for emerald fields alone,
With ambient streams more pure and bright   50
Than fabled Cytherea's zone
Glittering before the Thunderer's sight,
Is to my heart of hearts endeared
The ground where we were born and reared !

Hail, ancient Manners ! sure defence,   55
Where they survive, of wholesome laws ;
Remnants of love whose modest sense
Thus into narrow room withdraws ;
Hail, Usages of pristine mould,
And ye that guard them, Mountains old !   60

Bear with me, Brother ! quench the thought
That slights this passion, or condemns ;
If thee fond Fancy ever brought
From the proud margin of the Thames,
And Lambeth's venerable towers,   65
To humbler streams, and greener bowers.

Yes, they can make, who fail to find,
Short leisure even in busiest days ;
Moments, to cast a look behind,
And profit by those kindly rays   70
That through the clouds do sometimes steal,
And all the far-off past reveal.

Hence, while the imperial City's din
Beats frequent on thy satiate ear,
A pleased attention I may win   75
To agitations less severe,
That neither overwhelm nor cloy,
But fill the hollow vale with joy !

"BLEAK SEASON WAS IT, TURBULENT AND WILD"

BLEAK season was it, turbulent and wild,
When hitherward we journeyed, side by side,
Through bursts of sunshine and through flying
    showers,
Paced the long Vales, how long they were, and yet
How fast that length of way was left behind,   5
Wensley's rich Vale and Sedbergh's naked heights.
The frosty wind, as if to make amends
For its keen breath, was aiding to our steps,
And drove us onward as two ships at sea ;
Or, like two birds, companions in mid-air,   10
Parted and reunited by the blast.
Stern was the face of nature ; we rejoiced
In that stern countenance ; for our souls thence
    drew
A feeling of their strength.   The naked trees,
The icy brooks, as on we passed, appeared   15
To question us, "Whence come ye ?   To what
    end ? "

Chronicles of the Vale

On that tall pike
(It is the loneliest place of all these hills)
There were two springs which bubbled side by side,
As if they had been made that they might be
Companions for each other : the huge crag   5
Was rent with lightning—one hath disappeared ;
The other, left behind, is flowing still.
For accidents and changes such as these,
We want not store of them ;—a waterspout
Will bring down half a mountain ; what a feast   10
For folks that wander up and down like you,
To see an acre's breadth of that wide cliff
One roaring cataract ! a sharp May-storm
Will come with loads of January snow,
And in one night send twenty score of sheep   15
To feed the ravens ; or a shepherd dies
By some untoward death among the rocks :
The ice breaks up and sweeps away a bridge ;
A wood is felled :—and then for our own homes !
A child is born or christened, a field ploughed,   20
A daughter sent to service, a web spun,
The old house-clock is decked with a new face ;
And hence, so far from wanting facts or dates
To chronicle the time, we all have here
A pair of diaries,—one serving, Sir,   25
For the whole dale, and one for each fire-side—
Yours was a stranger's judgment : for historians,
Commend me to these valleys !

(The Brothers, 139-66)

Nature's Door

THE priests are from their altars thrust ;
Temples are levelled with the dust ;
And solemn rites and awful forms
Founder amid fanatic storms.
Yet evermore, through years renewed   5
In undisturbed vicissitude
Of seasons balancing their flight
On the swift wings of day and night,
Kind Nature keeps a heavenly door
Wide open for the scattered Poor.   10
Where flower-breathed incense to the skies
Is wafted in mute harmonies ;
And ground fresh-cloven by the plough
Is fragrant with a humbler vow ;
Where birds and brooks from leafy dells   15
Chime forth unwearied canticles,
And vapours magnify and spread
The glory of the sun's bright head—
Still constant in her worship, still
Conforming to the eternal Will,   20
Whether men sow or reap the fields,
Divine monition Nature yields,
That not by bread alone we live,
Or what a hand of flesh can give ;
That every day should leave some part   25
Free for a sabbath of the heart :
So shall the seventh be truly blest,
From morn to eve, with hallowed rest.

(*Devotional Incitements*, 50-77)

A Grasmere Shepherd

UPON the forest-side in Grasmere Vale
There dwelt a Shepherd, Michael was his name ;
An old man, stout of heart, and strong of limb.
His bodily frame had been from youth to age
Of an unusual strength : his mind was keen,   5
Intense, and frugal, apt for all affairs,
And in his shepherd's calling he was prompt
And watchful more than ordinary men.
Hence had he learned the meaning of all winds,
Of blasts of every tone ; and oftentimes,   10
When others heeded not, He heard the South
Make subterraneous music, like the noise
Of bagpipers on distant Highland hills.
The Shepherd, at such warning, of his flock
Bethought him, and he to himself would say,   15
" The winds are now devising work for me ! "
And, truly, at all times, the storm, that drives
The traveller to a shelter, summoned him
Up to the mountains : he had been alone
Amid the heart of many thousand mists,   20
That came to him, and left him, on the heights.
So lived he till his eightieth year was past.
And grossly that man errs, who should suppose
That the green valleys, and the streams and rocks,
Were things indifferent to the Shepherd's thoughts. 25
Fields, where with cheerful spirits he had breathed
The common air ; hills, which with vigorous step
He had so often climbed ; which had impressed
So many incidents upon his mind
Of hardship, skill or courage, joy or fear ;   30
Which, like a book, preserved the memory

Of the dumb animals, whom he had saved,
Had fed or sheltered, linking to such acts
The certainty of honourable gain ;
Those fields, those hills—what could they less? had laid 35
Strong hold on his affections, were to him
A pleasurable feeling of blind love,
The pleasure which there is in life itself.

(Michael, 40-77)

ANIMAL TRANQUILLITY AND DECAY

THE little hedgerow birds,
That peck along the road, regard him not.
He travels on, and in his face, his step,
His gait, is one expression : every limb,
His look and bending figure, all bespeak   5
A man who does not move with pain, but moves
With thought.—He is insensibly subdued
To settled quiet : he is one by whom
All effort seems forgotten ; one to whom
Long patience hath such mild composure given,   10
That patience now doth seem a thing of which
He hath no need.   He is by nature led
To peace so perfect that the young behold
With envy, what the Old Man hardly feels.

THE SMALL CELANDINE

THERE is a Flower, the lesser Celandine,
That shrinks, like many more, from cold and rain ;
And, the first moment that the sun may shine,
Bright as the sun himself, 'tis out again !

When hailstones have been falling, swarm on swarm, 5
Or blasts the green field and the trees distrest,
Oft have I seen it muffled up from harm,
In close self-shelter, like a Thing at rest.

But lately, one rough day, this Flower I passed
And recognised it, though an altered form, 10
Now standing forth an offering to the blast,
And buffeted at will by rain and storm.

I stopped, and said with inly-muttered voice,
" It doth not love the shower, nor seek the cold :
This neither is its courage nor its choice, 15
But its necessity in being old.

" The sunshine may not cheer it, nor the dew ;
It cannot help itself in its decay ;
Stiff in its members, withered, changed of hue."
And, in my spleen, I smiled that it was grey. 20

To be a Prodigal's Favourite—then, worse truth,
A Miser's Pensioner—behold our lot !
O Man, that from thy fair and shining youth
Age might but take the things Youth needed not !

The Mountain Daisy

So fair, so sweet, withal so sensitive,
Would that the little Flowers were born to live,
Conscious of half the pleasure which they give ;

That to this mountain-daisy's self were known
The beauty of its star-shaped shadow, thrown   5
On the smooth surface of this naked stone !

And what if hence a bold desire should mount
High as the Sun, that he could take account
Of all that issues from his glorious fount !

So might he ken how by his sovereign aid   10
These delicate companionships are made ;
And how he rules the pomp of light and shade ;

And were the Sister-power that shines by night
So privileged, what a countenance of delight
Would through the clouds break forth on human
        sight !   15

Fond fancies ! wheresoe'er shall turn thine eye
On earth, air, ocean, or the starry sky,
Converse with Nature in pure sympathy ;

All vain desires, all lawless wishes quelled,
Be Thou to love and praise alike impelled,   20
Whatever boon is granted or withheld.

NUTTING

——————————It seems a day
(I speak of one from many singled out)
One of those heavenly days that cannot die ;
When, in the eagerness of boyish hope,
I left our cottage-threshold, sallying forth   5
With a huge wallet o'er my shoulders slung,
A nutting-crook in hand ; and turned my steps
Tow'rd some far-distant wood, a Figure quaint,
Tricked out in proud disguise of cast-off weeds
Which for that service had been husbanded,   10
By exhortation of my frugal Dame—
Motley accoutrement, of power to smile
At thorns, and brakes, and brambles,—and in truth
More ragged than need was !   O'er pathless rocks,
Through beds of matted fern, and tangled thickets,   15
Forcing my way, I came to one dear nook
Unvisited, where not a broken bough
Drooped with its withered leaves, ungracious sign
Of devastation ; but the hazels rose
Tall and erect, with tempting clusters hung,   20
A virgin scene !—A little while I stood,
Breathing with such suppression of the heart
As joy delights in ; and with wise restraint
Voluptuous, fearless of a rival, eyed
The banquet ;—or beneath the trees I sate   25
Among the flowers, and with the flowers I played ;
A temper known to those who, after long
And weary expectation, have been blest
With sudden happiness beyond all hope.
Perhaps it was a bower beneath whose leaves   30
The violets of five seasons re-appear

And fade, unseen by any human eye ;
Where fairy water-breaks do murmur on
For ever ; and I saw the sparkling foam,
And with my cheek on one of those green stones   35
That, fleeced with moss, under the shady trees,
Lay round me, scattered like a flock of sheep—
I heard the murmur and the murmuring sound,
In that sweet mood when pleasure loves to pay
Tribute to ease ; and, of its joy secure,   40
The heart luxuriates with indifferent things,
Wasting its kindliness on stocks and stones,
And on the vacant air.   Then up I rose,
And dragged to earth both branch and bough, with crash
And merciless ravage : and the shady nook   45
Of hazels, and the green and mossy bower,
Deformed and sullied, patiently gave up
Their quiet being : and unless I now
Confound my present feelings with the past,
Ere from the mutilated bower I turned   50
Exulting, rich beyond the wealth of kings,
I felt a sense of pain when I beheld
The silent trees, and saw the intruding sky.—
Then, dearest Maiden, move along these shades
In gentleness of heart ; with gentle hand   55
Touch—for there is a spirit in the woods.

A NIGHT-PIECE

————The sky is overcast
With a continuous cloud of texture close,
Heavy and wan, all whitened by the Moon,
Which through that veil is indistinctly seen,

A dull, contracted circle, yielding light   5
So feebly spread that not a shadow falls,
Chequering the ground—from rock, plant, tree, or tower.
At length a pleasant instantaneous gleam
Startles the pensive traveller while he treads
His lonesome path, with unobserving eye   10
Bent earthwards ; he looks up—the clouds are split
Asunder,—and above his head he sees
The clear Moon, and the glory of the heavens.
There in a black-blue vault she sails along,
Followed by multitudes of stars, that, small   15
And sharp, and bright, along the dark abyss
Drive as she drives : how fast they wheel away,
Yet vanish not !—the wind is in the tree,
But they are silent ;—still they roll along
Immeasurably distant ; and the vault,   20
Built round by those white clouds, enormous clouds,
Still deepens its unfathomable depth.
At length the Vision closes ; and the mind,
Not undisturbed by the delight it feels,
Which slowly settles into peaceful calm,   25
Is left to muse upon the solemn scene.

THE SIMPLON PASS

———Brook and road
Were fellow-travellers in this gloomy Pass,
And with them did we journey several hours
At a slow step.   The immeasurable height
Of woods decaying, never to be decayed,   5
The stationary blasts of waterfalls,
And in the narrow rent, at every turn,
Winds thwarting winds bewildered and forlorn,

The torrents shooting from the clear blue sky,
The rocks that muttered close upon our ears,   10
Black drizzling crags that spake by the wayside
As if a voice were in them, the sick sight
And giddy prospect of the raving stream,
The unfettered clouds and region of the
    heavens,
Tumult and peace, the darkness and the light—   15
Were all like workings of one mind, the features
Of the same face, blossoms upon one tree,
Characters of the great Apocalypse,
The types and symbols of Eternity,
Of first, and last, and midst, and without end.   20

Fragment from "The Recluse"

On Man, on Nature, and on Human Life,
Musing in solitude, I oft perceive
Fair trains of imagery before me rise,
Accompanied by feelings of delight
Pure, or with no unpleasing sadness mixed ;   5
And I am conscious of affecting thoughts
And dear remembrances, whose presence soothes
Or elevates the Mind, intent to weigh
The good and evil of our mortal state.
—To these emotions, whencesoe'er they come,   10
Whether from breath of outward circumstance,
Or from the Soul—an impulse to herself—
I would give utterance in numerous verse.
Of Truth, of Grandeur, Beauty, Love, and Hope,
And melancholy Fear subdued by Faith ;   15
Of blessèd consolations in distress ;
Of moral strength, and intellectual Power ;

Of joy in widest commonalty spread ;
Of the individual Mind that keeps her own
Inviolate retirement, subject there   20
To Conscience only, and the law supreme
Of that Intelligence which governs all—
I sing :—' fit audience let me find though few ! '

   .   .   .   .

—Beauty—a living Presence of the earth,
Surpassing the most fair ideal Forms   25
Which craft of delicate Spirits hath composed
From earth's materials—waits upon my steps ;
Pitches her tents before me as I move,
An hourly neighbour.   Paradise, and groves
Elysian, Fortunate Fields—like those of old   30
Sought in the Atlantic Main—why should they be
A history only of departed things,
Or a mere fiction of what never was ?
For the discerning intellect of Man,
When wedded to this goodly universe   35
In love and holy passion, shall find these
A simple produce of the common day.
—I, long before the blissful hour arrives,
Would chant, in lonely peace, the spousal verse
Of this great consummation :—and, by words   40
Which speak of nothing more than what we are,
Would I arouse the sensual from their sleep
Of Death, and win the vacant and the vain
To noble raptures.

(From the Preface to
The Excursion, 1-23 ; 42-62)

ELEGIAC STANZAS

SUGGESTED BY A PICTURE OF PEELE CASTLE, IN A
STORM, PAINTED BY SIR GEORGE BEAUMONT

I WAS thy neighbour once, thou rugged Pile !
Four summer weeks I dwelt in sight of thee :
I saw thee every day ; and all the while
Thy Form was sleeping on a glassy sea.

So pure the sky, so quiet was the air !   5
So like, so very like, was day to day !
Whene'er I looked, thy Image still was there ;
It trembled, but it never passed away.

How perfect was the calm ! it seemed no sleep ;
No mood, which season takes away, or brings :   10
I could have fancied that the mighty Deep
Was even the gentlest of all gentle Things.

Ah ! THEN, if mine had been the Painter's hand,
To express what then I saw ; and add the gleam,
The light that never was, on sea or land,   15
The consecration, and the Poet's dream ;

I would have planted thee, thou hoary Pile
Amid a world how different from this !
Beside a sea that could not cease to smile ;
On tranquil land, beneath a sky of bliss.   20

Thou shouldst have seemed a treasure-house divine
Of peaceful years ; a chronicle of heaven ;—
Of all the sunbeams that did ever shine
The very sweetest had to thee been given.

A Picture had it been of lasting ease,   25
Elysian quiet, without toil or strife ;
No motion but the moving tide, a breeze,
Or merely silent Nature's breathing life.

(Excerpt—see note)

A POET'S EPITAPH

ART thou a Statist in the van
Of public conflicts trained and bred ?
—First learn to love one living man ;
Then may'st thou think upon the dead.

A Lawyer art thou ?—draw not nigh !   5
Go, carry to some fitter place
The keenness of that practised eye,
The hardness of that sallow face.

Art thou a Man of purple cheer ?
A rosy Man, right plump to see ?   10
Approach ; yet, Doctor, not too near,
This grave no cushion is for thee.

Or art thou one of gallant pride,
A Soldier and no man of chaff ?
Welcome !—but lay thy sword aside,   15
And lean upon a peasant's staff.

Physician art thou ?—one, all eyes,
Philosopher !—a fingering slave,
One that would peep and botanise
Upon his mother's grave ?   20

Wrapt closely in thy sensual fleece,
O turn aside,—and take, I pray,
That he below may rest in peace,
Thy ever-dwindling soul, away !

A Moralist perchance appears ;   25
Led, Heaven knows how ! to this poor sod :
And he has neither eyes nor ears ;
Himself his world, and his own God ;

One to whose smooth-rubbed soul can cling
Nor form, nor feeling, great or small ;   30
A reasoning, self-sufficing thing,
An intellectual All-in-all !

Shut close the door ; press down the latch ;
Sleep in thy intellectual crust ;
Nor lose ten tickings of thy watch   35
Near this unprofitable dust.

But who is He, with modest looks,
And clad in homely russet brown ?
He murmurs near the running brooks
A music sweeter than their own.   40

He is retired as noontide dew,
Or fountain in a noon-day grove ;
And you must love him, ere to you
He will seem worthy of your love.

The outward shows of sky and earth,   45
Of hill and valley, he has viewed ;
And impulses of deeper birth
Have come to him in solitude.

In common things that round us lie
Some random truths he can impart,— 50
The harvest of a quiet eye
That broods and sleeps on his own heart.

But he is weak ; both Man and Boy,
Hath been an idler in the land ;
Contented if he might enjoy 55
The things which others understand.

—Come hither in thy hour of strength ;
Come, weak as is a breaking wave !
Here stretch thy body at full length ;
Or build thy house upon this grave. 60

TINTERN ABBEY

LINES COMPOSED A FEW MILES ABOVE TINTERN ABBEY,
ON REVISITING THE BANKS OF THE WYE DURING A
TOUR. JULY 13, 1798.

FIVE years have past ; five summers, with the length
Of five long winters ! and again I hear
These waters, rolling from their mountain-springs
With a soft inland murmur.—Once again
Do I behold these steep and lofty cliffs, 5
That on a wild secluded scene impress
Thoughts of more deep seclusion ; and connect
The landscape with the quiet of the sky.
The day is come when I again repose
Here, under this dark sycamore, and view 10
These plots of cottage-ground, these orchard-tufts,
Which at this season, with their unripe fruits,

Are clad in one green hue, and lose themselves
'Mid groves and copses.   Once again I see
These hedge-rows, hardly hedge-rows, little lines   15
Of sportive wood run wild : these pastoral farms,
Green to the very door : and wreaths of smoke
Sent up, in silence, from among the trees !
With some uncertain notice, as might seem
Of vagrant dwellers in the houseless woods,   20
Or of some Hermit's cave, where by his fire
The Hermit sits alone.

                  These beauteous forms,
Through a long absence, have not been to me
As is a landscape to a blind man's eye :
But oft, in lonely rooms, and 'mid the din   25
Of towns and cities, I have owed to them,
In hours of weariness, sensations sweet,
Felt in the blood, and felt along the heart ;
And passing even into my purer mind,
With tranquil restoration :—feelings too   30
Of unremembered pleasure : such, perhaps,
As have no slight or trivial influence
On that best portion of a good man's life,
His little, nameless, unremembered, acts
Of kindness and of love.   Nor less, I trust,   35
To them I may have owed another gift,
Of aspect more sublime ; that blessed mood,
In which the burthen of the mystery,
In which the heavy and the weary weight
Of all this unintelligible world,   40
Is lightened :—that serene and blessed mood,
In which the affections gently lead us on,—
Until, the breath of this corporeal frame
And even the motion of our human blood

Almost suspended, we are laid asleep   45
In body, and become a living soul :
While with an eye made quiet by the power
Of harmony, and the deep power of joy,
We see into the life of things.

                        If this
Be but a vain belief, yet, oh ! how oft—   50
In darkness and amid the many shapes
Of joyless daylight ; when the fretful stir
Unprofitable, and the fever of the world,
Have hung upon the beatings of my heart—
How oft, in spirit, have I turned to thee,   55
O sylvan Wye ! thou wanderer thro' the woods,
How often has my spirit turned to thee !

   And now, with gleams of half-extinguished thought,
With many recognitions dim and faint,
And somewhat of a sad perplexity,   60
The picture of the mind revives again :
While here I stand, not only with the sense
Of present pleasure, but with pleasing thoughts
That in this moment there is life and food
For future years.   And so I dare to hope,   65
Though changed, no doubt, from what I was when first
I came among these hills ; when like a roe
I bounded o'er the mountains, by the sides
Of the deep rivers, and the lonely streams,
Wherever nature led : more like a man   70
Flying from something that he dreads than one
Who sought the thing he loved.   For nature then
(The coarser pleasures of my boyish days,
And their glad animal movements all gone by)
To me was all in all.—I cannot paint   75
What then I was.   The sounding cataract

Haunted me like a passion : the tall rock,
The mountain, and the deep and gloomy wood,
Their colours and their forms, were then to me
An appetite ; a feeling and a love,   80
That had no need of a remoter charm,
By thought supplied, nor any interest
Unborrowed from the eye.—That time is past,
And all its aching joys are now no more,
And all its dizzy raptures.   Not for this   85
Faint I, nor mourn nor murmur ; other gifts
Have followed ; for such loss, I would believe,
Abundant recompense. For I have learned
To look on nature, not as in the hour
Of thoughtless youth ; but hearing oftentimes   90
The still, sad music of humanity,
Nor harsh nor grating, though of ample power
To chasten and subdue.   And I have felt
A presence that disturbs me with the joy
Of elevated thoughts ; a sense sublime   95
Of something far more deeply interfused,
Whose dwelling is the light of setting suns,
And the round ocean and the living air,
And the blue sky, and in the mind of man :
A motion and a spirit, that impels   100
All thinking things, all objects of all thought,
And rolls through all things.   Therefore am I still
A lover of the meadows and the woods,
And mountains ; and of all that we behold
From this green earth ; of all the mighty world   105
Of eye, and ear,—both what they half create,
And what perceive ; well pleased to recognise
In nature and the language of the sense
The anchor of my purest thoughts, the nurse,
The guide, the guardian of my heart, and soul   110

Of all my moral being.
                  Nor perchance,
If I were not thus taught, should I the more
Suffer my genial spirits to decay :
For thou art with me here upon the banks
Of this fair river ; thou my dearest Friend,   115
My dear, dear Friend ; and in thy voice I catch
The language of my former heart, and read
My former pleasures in the shooting lights
Of thy wild eyes.   Oh ! yet a little while
May I behold in thee what I was once,   120
My dear, dear Sister ! and this prayer I make,
Knowing that Nature never did betray
The heart that loved her ; 'tis her privilege,
Through all the years of this our life, to lead
From joy to joy : for she can so inform   125
The mind that is within us, so impress
With quietness and beauty, and so feed
With lofty thoughts, that neither evil tongues,
Rash judgments, nor the sneers of selfish men,
Nor greetings where no kindness is, nor all   130
The dreary intercourse of daily life,
Shall e'er prevail against us, or disturb
Our cheerful faith, that all which we behold
Is full of blessings.   Therefore let the moon
Shine on thee in thy solitary walk ;   135
And let the misty mountain-winds be free
To blow against thee : and, in after years,
When these wild ecstasies shall be matured
Into a sober pleasure ; when thy mind
Shall be a mansion for all lovely forms,   140
Thy memory be as a dwelling-place
For all sweet sounds and harmonies ; oh ! then,
If solitude, or fear, or pain, or grief,

Should be thy portion, with what healing thoughts
Of tender joy wilt thou remember me,   145
And these my exhortations !   Nor, perchance—
If I should be where I no more can hear
Thy voice, nor catch from thy wild eyes these gleams
Of past existence—wilt thou then forget
That on the banks of this delightful stream   150
We stood together ; and that I, so long
A worshipper of Nature, hither came
Unwearied in that service : rather say
With warmer love—oh ! with far deeper zeal
Of holier love.   Nor wilt thou then forget   155
That after many wanderings, many years
Of absence, these steep woods and lofty cliffs,
And this green pastoral landscape, were to me
More dear, both for themselves and for thy sake !

ODE TO DUTY

" Jam non consilio bonus, sed more eò perductus, ut non
tantum rectè facere possim, sed nisi rectè facere non possim."

STERN Daughter of the Voice of God !
O Duty ! if that name thou love
Who art a light to guide, a rod
To check the erring, and reprove ;
Thou, who art victory and law   5
When empty terrors overawe ;
From vain temptations dost set free ;
And calm'st the weary strife of frail humanity !

There are who ask not if thine eye
Be on them ; who, in love and truth,   10
Where no misgiving is, rely
Upon the genial sense of youth :

Glad Hearts ! without reproach or blot ;
Who do thy work, and know it not :
Oh ! if through confidence misplaced   15
They fail, thy saving arms, dread Power ! around
     them cast.

Serene will be our days and bright,
And happy will our nature be,
When love is an unerring light,
And joy its own security.   20
And they a blissful course may hold
Even now, who, not unwisely bold,
Live in the spirit of this creed ;
Yet seek thy firm support, according to their
     need.

I, loving freedom, and untried ;   25
No sport of every random gust,
Yet being to myself a guide,
Too blindly have reposed my trust :
And oft, when in my heart was heard
Thy timely mandate, I deferred   30
The task, in smoother walks to stray ;
But thee I now would serve more strictly, if I
     may.

Through no disturbance of my soul,
Or strong compunction in me wrought,
I supplicate for thy control ;   35
But in the quietness of thought :
Me this unchartered freedom tires ;
I feel the weight of chance-desires :
My hopes no more must change their name,
I long for a repose that ever is the same.   40

Stern Lawgiver! yet thou dost wear
The Godhead's most benignant grace;
Nor know we anything so fair
As is the smile upon thy face:
Flowers laugh before thee on their beds   45
And fragrance in thy footing treads;
Thou dost preserve the stars from wrong;
And the most ancient heavens, through Thee, are
    fresh and strong.

To humbler functions, awful Power!
I call thee: I myself commend   50
Unto thy guidance from this hour;
Oh, let my weakness have an end!
Give unto me, made lowly wise,
The spirit of self-sacrifice;
The confidence of reason give;   55
And in the light of truth thy Bondman let me
    live!

ODE

ON INTIMATIONS OF IMMORTALITY FROM RECOLLECTIONS OF EARLY CHILDHOOD

The Child is father of the Man ;
And I could wish my days to be
Bound each to each by natural piety.

I

THERE was a time when meadow, grove, and stream,
 The earth, and every common sight,
   To me did seem
  Apparelled in celestial light,
The glory and the freshness of a dream.   5
It is not now as it hath been of yore ;—
  Turn wheresoe'er I may,
   By night or day,
The things which I have seen I now can see no
 more.

II

 The Rainbow comes and goes,   10
 And lovely is the Rose,
 The Moon doth with delight
Look round her when the heavens are bare,
 Waters on a starry night
  Are beautiful and fair ;   15
 The sunshine is a glorious birth ;
 But yet I know, where'er I go,
That there hath past away a glory from the earth.

14 M

III

Now, while the birds thus sing a joyous song,
    And while the young lambs bound   20
      As to the tabor's sound,
To me alone there came a thought of grief :
A timely utterance gave that thought relief,
    And I again am strong :
The cataracts blow their trumpets from the steep ;   25
  No more shall grief of mine the season wrong ;
  I hear the Echoes through the mountains throng,
The Winds come to me from the fields of sleep,
    And all the earth is gay ;
      Land and sea   30
   Give themselves up to jollity,
    And with the heart of May
Doth every Beast keep holiday ;—
     Thou child of joy,
Shout round me, let me hear thy shouts, thou happy
    Shepherd-boy !   35

IV

Ye blessèd Creatures, I have heard the call
    Ye to each other make ; I see
The heavens laugh with you in your jubilee ;
    My heart is at your festival,
    My head hath its coronal,   40
The fulness of your bliss, I feel—I feel it all.
     Oh evil day ! if I were sullen
    While Earth herself is adorning,
     This sweet May-morning,
    And the Children are culling   45
     On every side,
In a thousand valleys far and wide,

Fresh flowers ; while the sun shines warm,
And the Babe leaps up on his Mother's arm :—
   I hear, I hear, with joy I hear !   50
  —But there's a Tree, of many, one,
A single Field which I have looked upon,
Both of them speak of something that is gone :
    The Pansy at my feet
    Doth the same tale repeat :   55
Whither is fled the visionary gleam ?
Where is it now, the glory and the dream.

      v

Our birth is but a sleep and a forgetting :
The Soul that rises with us, our life's Star,
   Hath had elsewhere its setting,   60
    And cometh from afar :
  Not in entire forgetfulness,
  And not in utter nakedness,
But trailing clouds of glory do we come
   From God, who is our home :   65
Heaven lies about us in our infancy !
Shades of the prison-house begin to close
   Upon the growing Boy,
But He beholds the light, and whence it flows,
   He sees it in his joy ;   70
The Youth, who daily farther from the east
  Must travel, still is Nature's Priest,
   And by the vision splendid
   Is on his way attended ;
At length the Man perceives it die away,   75
And fade into the light of common day.

VI

Earth fills her lap with pleasures of her own ;
Yearnings she hath in her own natural kind,
And, even with something of a Mother's mind,
   And no unworthy aim,   80
  The homely Nurse doth all she can
To make her Foster-child, her Inmate Man,
   Forget the glories he hath known,
And that imperial palace whence he came.

VII

Behold the Child among his new-born blisses, 85
 A six years' Darling of a pigmy size !
 See, where 'mid work of his own hand he lies,
Fretted by sallies of his mother's kisses,
 With light upon him from his father's eyes !
See, at his feet, some little plan or chart, 90
Some fragment from his dream of human life,
Shaped by himself with newly-learned art ;
   A wedding or a festival,
   A mourning or a funeral ;
    And this hath now his heart, 95
   And unto this he frames his song :
    Then will he fit his tongue
To dialogues of business, love, or strife :
    But it will not be long
    Ere this be thrown aside, 100
    And with new joy and pride
The little Actor cons another part ;
Filling from time to time his " humorous stage "
With all the Persons, down to palsied Age,
That life brings with her in her equipage ; 105
   As if his whole vocation
   Were endless imitation.

The child's games are make-believe.

VIII

Thou, whose exterior semblance doth belie
     Thy Soul's immensity ;
Thou best Philosopher who yet dost keep   110
Thy heritage, thou Eye among the blind,
That, deaf and silent, read'st the eternal deep,
Haunted for ever by the eternal mind,—
     Mighty Prophet ! Seer blest !
     On whom those truths do rest,   115
Which we are toiling all our lives to find,
In darkness lost, the darkness of the grave ;
Thou, over whom thy Immortality
Broods like the Day, a Master o'er a Slave,
A presence which is not to be put by ;   120
     [To whom the grave
Is but a lonely bed without the sense or sight
     Of day or the warm light,
A place of thought where we in waiting lie ;]
Thou little Child, yet glorious in the might   125
Of heaven-born freedom on thy being's height,
Why with such earnest pains dost thou provoke
The years to bring the inevitable yoke,
Thus blindly with thy blessedness at strife ?
Full soon thy Soul shall have her earthly freight,   130
And custom lie upon thee with a weight,
Heavy as frost, and deep almost as life !

IX

     O joy ! that in our embers
     Is something that doth live,
     That nature yet remembers   135
     What was so fugitive !
The thought of our past years in me doth breed
Perpetual benediction : not indeed

For that which is most worthy to be blest ;
Delight and liberty, the simple creed   140
Of Childhood, whether busy or at rest,
With new-fledged hope still fluttering in his
                    breast :—
          Not for these I raise
          The song of thanks and praise ;
But for those obstinate questionings   145
     Of sense and outward things,
     Fallings from us, vanishings ;
     Blank misgivings of a Creature
Moving about in worlds not realised,
High instincts before which our mortal Nature   150
Did tremble like a guilty Thing surprised :
     But for those first affections,
     Those shadowy recollections,
          Which, be they what they may,
Are yet the fountain-light of all our day,   155
Are yet a master-light of all our seeing ;
     Uphold us, cherish, and have power to make
Our noisy years seem moments in the being
     Of the eternal Silence : truths that wake,
          To perish never :   160
Which neither listlessness, nor mad endeavour,
          Nor man nor Boy,
Nor all that is at enmity with joy,
Can utterly abolish or destroy !
     Hence in a season of calm weather   165
          Though inland far we be,
Our souls have sight of that immortal sea
          Which brought us hither,
          Can in a moment travel thither,
And see the Children sport upon the shore,   170
And hear the mighty waters rolling evermore.

X

Then sing, ye Birds, sing, sing a joyous song !
   And let the young Lambs bound
   As to the tabor's sound !
 We in thought will join your throng,   175
   Ye that pipe and ye that play,
   Ye that through your hearts to-day
   Feel the gladness of the May !
What though the radiance which was once so
  bright
Be now for ever taken from my sight,   180
 Though nothing can bring back the hour
Of splendour in the grass, of glory in the flower ;
   We will grieve not, rather find
   Strength in what remains behind ;
   In the primal sympathy   185
   Which having been must ever be ;
   In the soothing thoughts that spring
   Out of human suffering ;
   In the faith that looks through death,
 In years that bring the philosophic mind. 190

XI

And O, ye Fountains, Meadows, Hills, and Groves,
Forebode not any severing of our loves !
Yet in my heart of hearts I feel your might ;
I only have relinquished one delight
To live beneath your more habitual sway.   195
I love the Brooks which down their channels fret,
Even more than when I tripped lightly as they ;
The innocent brightness of a new-born Day
   Is lovely yet ;

The Clouds that gather round the setting sun   200
Do take a sober colouring from an eye
That hath kept watch o'er man's mortality;
Another race hath been, and other palms are won.
Thanks to the human heart by which we live,
Thanks to its tenderness, its joys, and fears,   205
To me the meanest flower that blows can give
Thoughts that do often lie too deep for tears.

NOTES

CHIEF DATES

1770   Wordsworth born (April 7th).

        1771   Dorothy Wordsworth born.

        1772   Coleridge born.

1778   To school at Hawkshead.   Death of Mother.

        1783 Death of father.

1786   Writes early poems.

1787   To Cambridge.

1790   First visit to France, walking tour in Long Vacation.

1791   B.A. Camb.   Wanders.   North Wales, etc.

1792   Orleans ; second visit to France.   Revolutionary friends.

1793   Wandering in England and Wales.   Early work publ.

1795   Legacy (Calvert, £900).   Settles with Dorothy in Dorset. Meets Coleridge.

1798   *Lyrical Ballads* (Alfoxden).   *Prelude* begun.   Visits Germany (Sept., 1798–April, 1799).

1799   Settles with Dorothy at Dove Cottage, Grasmere.

1802   Marries Mary Hutchinson (after visit with sister to Calais).

1803   First tour in Scotland.

        1805   Brother, John W., lost at sea.

1807   (At Coleorton).   *Poems in Two Volumes* (badly reviewed).

1808   Allan Bank, Grasmere.

1813   Government appointment, Stamp-distributor, Westmorland.   Moves to Rydal Mount.

1815   First collective edition of *Poems.*

1843   Poet-Laureate.

1850   Wordsworth died.

NOTES

(The heavy figures at the beginning of individual notes refer to pages, the light figures to lines. It is hoped that some of the notes will suggest interesting investigation in the complete Works and in other sources named in the 'Guide for Reading.')

THE PRELUDE

To a reader unacquainted with Wordsworth's literary history, it must seem odd that the poet's greatest work was not published until after his death and that, when it did appear, it was called *The Prelude*. It consisted (1850) of fourteen books, amounting to nearly eight thousand lines in all. Its full title was *The Prelude; or, Growth of a Poet's Mind*, and it dealt with Wordsworth's life and feelings from childhood, through student days and revolutionary strife, to a manhood of ardent vision and impassioned calm.

The main work was begun in 1798 and in 1805 it existed complete, in a slightly longer form, in note-books which were first edited and published by Professor de Sélincourt in 1926. Between 1806 and 1850 the poet made various revisions, sometimes moderating the outspokenness of his youthful sentiments, and often introducing a precise image in place of a vaguer expression. The study of these revisions affords valuable insight into the working of a poet's mind. The title, *Prelude*, of the posthumous publication, was given by Mrs Wordsworth, in fidelity to Wordsworth's intention, as shown by correspondence and as announced publicly in the Preface to the *Excursion* (1814). The *Prelude* was in fact to have been preparatory to a still larger poem in three parts, called the *Recluse*, wherein 'Man, Nature, and Society' were to be reflected in the mind of 'a poet living in retirement.' The whole he anticipated figuratively as 'a Gothic church' with the *Prelude* 'as the Ante-chapel' and his minor poems as 'the little cells, oratories, and sepulchral recesses, ordinarily included in those edifices.' Such was the grandiose scheme, characteristic of a very ambitious young poet, which had fired Wordsworth's purpose early in 1798.

The conception of so wide a philosophic unity was really more germane to the mind of Coleridge, and though he encouraged Wordsworth, only one part of this *Recluse*—the second, called the *Excursion* (1814)—was ever finished ; meanwhile the poem on which Wordsworth had thought to try out his powers, *i.e.* the *Prelude*, received the wealth of his fresh imagination ; and though the *Excursion* was thereby impoverished, that is no matter for regret, because the task of describing, in faithful and impassioned recollection, ' the Growth of a Poet's Mind ' was the best possible subject for Wordsworth's special genius ; indeed, the *Prelude* is unsurpassed in this kind in the literature of the world.

The unravelling of the detailed history of the *Prelude* could only be done in a large work of fine scholarship such as the Variorum Edition by Professor de Sélincourt. It is sufficient here to point out that, as was natural, Wordsworth could not at once place in their ultimate setting all the passages he wrote in his approach to his big task. Thus, the opening lines (p. 3) belong to a passage written in September, 1795, before he had the notion of the longer work; a long piece, *The Ruined Cottage*, written in spring 1798, went finally to the first book of the *Excursion* ; the fine lines eventually introducing the *Excursion* (*see* p. 124) were written about the same time, so was the fragment published separately called *The Old Cumberland Beggar*, and a passage in *Prelude*, iv (370-469) describing a strange encounter with a discharged soldier ; the boat episode (p. 6), ' There was a Boy'' (p. 18), and the skating reminiscence (p. 9), were probably done in Germany, autumn 1798, after interruption of the work by the Lyrical Ballads ; whereas *Nutting* (p. 121), written about the same time for the *Prelude*, could find no ultimate place there.

Books I and II were finished by the end of 1799, with various fragments that were to come in later Books. From 1800 to 1803 Wordsworth did comparatively little at this large work ; but from March 1804 he gradually extended his scope, and by June in the following year he had finished the nine thousand lines which were to be revised and pruned to the final form in which the *Prelude* appeared forty-six years later. The women of Wordsworth's household, his sister, his wife, and his sister-in-law, Sara Hutchinson, worked as patient amanuenses, copying his puzzling handwriting with extraordinary accuracy. The whole conception and soul's history was addressed to the mind of Coleridge: copies had been made for him by Dorothy and Sara, but it was not until their reunion at Coleorton in 1806-7 that Coleridge was to hear the complete reading from Wordsworth's lips.

He was deeply moved, and on the following day he gave tribute of immortality to his friend in the poem " To William Wordsworth."

> O great Bard !
> Ere yet that last strain dying awed the air,
> With stedfast eye I viewed thee in the choir
> Of ever-enduring men.

There is a letter from Wordsworth to Sir George Beaumont (1st May, 1805) which best contains Wordsworth's own quiet and steady view of the completion of his task.

> It will be . . . a thing unprecedented in literary history that a man should talk so much about himself. It is not self-conceit, as you will know well, that has induced me to do this, but real humility. I began the work because I was unprepared to treat of any more arduous subject, and diffident of my own powers. Here, at least, I hoped that to a certain degree I should be sure of succeeding, as I had nothing to do but describe what I had felt and thought; therefore could not easily be bewildered. This might certainly have been done in narrower compass by a man of more address; but I have done my best.—(*Letters*, Vol. I, 186).

In undertaking so large a work in Blank Verse, Wordsworth was devoutly conscious of his great predecessors and cherished an ambition to be the Milton of his age. He has not Milton's sonority nor, of course, his superb familiarity with classical imagination, and he has many bare, homely lines that have nothing to do with Milton's loftiness ; nevertheless, Wordsworth used Blank Verse as a vehicle of exalted and sustained feeling and, as Professor de Sélincourt says, the style in the *Prelude* takes on a Miltonic manner.

2 — These lines are from the *Song at the Feast of Brougham Castle* (1807) describing a Lord Clifford who had been a shepherd. They seem most apt to describe Wordsworth himself.

SELECTIONS FROM THE *PRELUDE*
Introduction

3 — These lines, opening the *Prelude*, were written in September, 1795, when Wordsworth set out from Bristol for Racedown, in Dorsetshire, his first home in reunion with his sister. This statement contradicts most editors, who have followed the *Advertisement* to the First Edition, which says that the *Prelude* was begun in 1799 ; but Professors Garrod and de Sélincourt have placed the matter beyond doubt.

3 1-3 breeze . . . half conscious of joy: nature's oneness with humanity is a characteristic theme (cf. *Lines in Early Spring*, 11-12, etc.)

3 6-7 escaped from the vast city : from January to September 1795 Wordsworth was in London, probably waiting for the settlement of the Calvert legacy (*cf.* Introduction, xvi).

3 14 The earth is all before me : an echo of Milton ' The world was all before them, where to choose ' (*Paradise Lost*, XII, 646).

3 17 wandering cloud : note the trust in nature, and also the image (*cf.* ' I wandered lonely as a cloud,' p. 51, and the second line of *Hart-Leap Well*, p. 99).

Derwent River

3 — The river flows through Derwentwater and Bassenthwaite and joins the Cocker under the walls of the Castle at Cockermouth, where Wordsworth was born.

4 5 along my dreams : note the mystical tendency of Wordsworth's preposition ' along ' (*cf.* ' felt along the heart'), *Tintern Abbey* (**130.**28).

4 6 holm : a small island, especially in a river.

Bathing

4 7 ragwort : yellow wild flower with ragged leaves—allied to groundsel, but larger.

4 8 Skiddaw : 4 miles N. of Keswick. Height 3054 feet.

Night Snares—and Nemesis

4 4 belovèd Vale : *i.e.* of Esthwaite, at the north-west end of which is Hawkshead. Wordsworth and his elder brother Richard entered school there at Whitsuntide, 1779.

5 10 springes : nooses, snares.

5 23 **Low breathings**: note that the admonition comes char-acteristically from nature and not from moral precept (cf. *With Trembling Oars*, p. 6; also *The Palfreys*, **14.**24).

Bird-Nesting

5 — Note the vividness of first-hand experience in the images —'I have hung,' 'almost suspended by the blast,' the 'loud dry wind,' the whirling clouds. The passage has a touch of the poet who managed to be 'first-hand' about everything. (Cf. *King Lear*, IV, vi, a passage quoted by Wordsworth elsewhere.)

A Dark Inscrutable Workmanship

6 1-2 **the immortal spirit grows like harmony**: cf. Introduc-tion, xxv (footnote), which passage should also be borne in mind when considering line 16.

6 16 **Severer interventions**: again this tendency to youthful paganism, referring to spirit powers (cf. also the end of *Nutting*, p. 122, 'there is a spirit in the woods').

6 17 **as best might suit her aim**: in the original (1805) Words-worth had written, with a sense of more definite intervention, 'and so she dealt with me.' He tried later to moderate passages such as might offend religious opinion.

With Trembling Oars

6 — This incident relates not to Esthwaite but to Ullswater. Wordsworth was staying at Patterdale on his way home for school holidays, and the episode is given in the discovered early version with local reference and more casual details. Professor de Sélincourt surmises that the 'huge peak' (**7.**19) was Black Crag (2000 feet).

6 1 **by her**: *i.e.* nature (*cf.* l. 12, above). (The lines from *Bathing*, p. 4, to the end of *Skating*, p. 10, are consecutive in *Prelude*, i.)

7 23 **instinct**: *i.e.* 'charged'—form adopted from Lat. past participle.

8 42 the comma after 'forms' is moved to the end of the line by Professor Garrod, an alteration confirmed by Professor de Sélincourt.

Nature's Dower

8 — The lines from here to the end of *Skating*, p. 10, were first published in Coleridge's Paper *The Friend* (1809).

8 14 A grandeur in the beatings of the heart : Wordsworth's extraordinary reverence for the mystery of common things is at once a strength and a danger. When, as here, he makes explicit his exalted emotion, the reader too is moved. But he was capable of seeing mystery enough in the mere dates on a child's tombstone and is sometimes in danger of neglecting to make his poetry more moving than bare statement.

School Days at Hawkshead

8 1-2 Nor . . . with stinted kindness : *see* Introduction, xiv. The boys boarding with cottage dames seem to have had little restraint as to hours (*cf.* 'both day and night,' l. 9, or 'I heeded not their summons,' **9.**4).

Skating

9 — This beautiful and exhilarating picture refers, of course, to boyish skating upon Esthwaite. Wordsworth still skated well at sixty, *see* Introduction, xxvi.

9 17-18 The leafless trees . . . tinkled : a delicate sound image noted by Wordsworth, whose senses of sight and of hearing were abnormally fine.

9 20 not unnoticed : double negatives of this kind are among Wordsworth's weaknesses (*cf.* **9.**23, 'not seldom,' etc.).

10 26 To cut across the reflex of a star : noted by G. H. Lewes and other critics as a particularly lovely line.

10 35-6 earth rolled . . . her diurnal round : *cf.* 'A slumber did my Spirit seal' (p. 70), written about the same time at Goslar.

Other Pastimes

11 21-30 Compare passages above-named, for the remarkable freedom of these Hawkshead boarders; *see* also p. 15, in particular. 'Beating minds' echoes possibly *The Tempest*, IV. i.

School-Time Meals

11 10-11 the Dame of the old grey stone : Wordsworth's Dame was Anne Tyson, who died in 1796, aged 83.

Rides

12 5 courteous inn-keeper : the earliest MSS. has 'cautious,' which seems more likely, where boys are concerned.

12 8 temple : Knight surmises Conishead Priory on Cartmel Sands.

12 10 large abbey : *i.e.* Furness, 21 miles from Hawkshead.

The Chauntry and the Wren

12 3 cross-legged knight : stone effigy on a crusader's tomb.

13 23 We beat with thundering hoofs the level sand : the identical line closes *Prelude*, Book X, which tells us how, years later, along those sands, Wordsworth heard the cry " Robespierre is dead ! "

The Palfreys

13 1 One Christmas time : *i.e.* 1783.

13 6 My brothers : *i.e.* Richard and John.

14 22 my three brothers : Christopher had been too young to join the others at school.

14 24-25 appeared a chastisement : again a silent admonition in natural symbols (*cf.* 5.23). The process leaves one to realize the reticence and depth of feeling of the lad who imagined it.

14 37 in such indisputable shapes : strongly reminiscent of *Hamlet*, I, iv, ' Thou comest in such a questionable shape.'

15 49 animate an hour of vacant ease : cf. ' *I wandered lonely* ' (52.20-21) :

> In vacant or in pensive mood
> They flash upon that inward eye . . .

Free, as a Boy to Walk Alone

Compare 8.1-2, 11.21-30, above, for this freedom.

15 6 a coming storm : Wordsworth's imagination was always deeply stirred by tempest (*cf.* l. 45 above, **14.**11, foot of p. 16, *Resolution and Independence*, p. 106, etc.).

15 10 visionary power : the message to the senses always has a larger inference (*cf.* top of p. 21) :

> visionary power
> Attends the motions of the viewless winds

For other instances, *see* foot of p. 29, top of p. 33, *Cuckoo*, 55.11.

Ye Mountains

16 — This is a suitable place to quote Prof. A. N. Whitehead, a modern philosopher who utters the following appreciation of traits which should be clear from the first dozen pages of these " Selections " :

> It is the brooding presence of the hills which haunts him. His theme is nature *in solido*, that is to say, he dwells on that mysterious

presence of surrounding things, which imposes itself on any separate element that we set up as an individual for its own sake. He always grasps the whole of nature as involved in the tonality of the particular instance.

16 13 That lowly bed : dealing with the same scene, a passage of 23 lines discovered by Professor de Sélincourt has more fanciful pageantry from young Wordsworth's mind :

> When in my bed I lay
> Alone in darkness, I have seen the gloom
> Peopled with shapes arrayed in hues more bright
> Than flowers or gems, or than the evening sky.

Gaiety, a Dawn and a Dedication

17 — This passage, like the last, relates to the first Cambridge vacation, spent at Hawkshead. The actual walk taken is a matter of speculation. One must not press the autobiographical interest too far. As Mr Herbert Read says, writing of the *Prelude*, " The personal has become the universal, and once in that free space, it is almost impossible to find the way back again to the limitations of person, place and time."

17 18 Grain-tinctured : formerly the dye-yielding *coccus* insects, *cf.* ' cochineal,' were thought to be a berry (*granum*), and ' grain ' came to indicate fast dye. Thus Olivia, of her complexion, ' 'Tis in grain, Sir : 'twill endure wind and weather.'— *Twelfth Night*, I, v.)

17 23 dear Friend : Coleridge.

Memory of a Kindred Spirit

18 — A passage written in Germany, autumn 1798, and first published in *Lyrical Ballads* (2nd Ed.), 1800. In one of the Fenwick Notes, Wordsworth recalls the boyish mimicry here described.

> This practice of making an instrument of their own fingers is known to most boys, though some are more skilful at it than others. William Raincock of Rayrigg, a fine spirited lad, took the lead of all my school-fellows in this art.

18 1 Research has shown that the ' Boy ' was probably one John Vickars; but that doesn't matter.

18 2 Winander : Winandermere was the old name for Windermere.

18 11 they would shout: Wordsworth's application of the word ' shout ' to bird-calls is rather striking (*cf.* ' thy two-fold shout I hear,' *Cuckoo* 55.6, see note).

18 16 Jocund din: reminiscent of ' lively din ' in Milton's *L'Allegro*, l. 49—where the use of ' jocund ' occurs, l. 94.

18 20-21 the voice of mountain torrents: Professor Dowden picked out this passage as most characteristic of Wordsworth's poetic sense of hearing. (*Cf.* also **32**.59-62 ; **129**.4, etc.)

18 22 unawares: *cf.* ' wise passiveness,' **43**.24.

The Drowned Man
(Also probably written in Germany)

19 1 the very week: *i.e.* after Whitsuntide, 1779.

19 16 a fish up-leaping: another example of Wordsworth's fine susceptibility to effects of sound.

19 24 Of trees and hills and water: classical austerity of selection, with lovely effect in the final bare substantive.

Defrauding Glory

20 — This holiday description is included to show Wordsworth's natural conscience towards open-air pursuits. Most boys find themselves in the reverse position : they defraud reading for sport.

Visionary Power

20 — The nurture of the spirit, drawn from the senses' assimilation of objects of natural beauty, finds fructification in poetry.

21 13 viewless winds: cf. *Measure for Measure*, III, i, " To be imprison'd in the viewless winds."

London

21 — Wordsworth's first considerable stay in London was in 1791, after leaving Cambridge. Little is known of his objects or movements then.

21 12-16 The standard editions, following 1850, punctuate this passage as below ; but the punctuation indicated in brackets ends the lines in the 1805 version, and makes better sense.

> Here, fronts of houses, like a title page, (no comma)
> With letters huge inscribed from top to toe ;

> Stationed above the door, like guardian saints,
> There, allegoric shapes, female or male, (semicolon)
> Or physiognomies of real men.   (comma)
> Land warriors, Kings, etc.

Two London Pictures

22 — The initial impulse in his feeling for general causes, for a nation or for a social state, usually came to Wordsworth in a stir of poetic sympathy for the suffering or the nobility of an individual. Compare, with these two pictures, the following one of the Shepherd, or of the 'hunger-bitten girl' (**25.**2); *cf.* also the Leech-gatherer (p. 108), Toussaint (p. 80), etc.

23 14 **As if admonished :** this whole passage affords a fine example of an effect upon the poet's spirit more profound in striking impression than any weight of ' secondary ' reason could make it (*cf.* Introduction, xxxiii-iv).

Home Country again—and the Shepherd

24 35 **In size a giant :** *cf.* Thomson, *Seasons* (*Autumn*, 722-725).

> Indistinct on earth,
> Seen through the turbid air, beyond the life
> Objects appear ; and, wildered o'er the waste
> The shepherd stalks gigantic.

25 44 **Chartreuse :** La Grande Chartreuse, founded about 1135, is the chief monastery of the Carthusian Order. It is situated in a wild, picturesque valley in the Department of Isère, about 13 m. North of Grenoble. Wordsworth visited it in 1790 with Robert Jones (*cf.* note on **31.**1) and there 'Rested within an awful solitude,' deeply moved (*Prelude*, vi, 414-478). One of Dorothy Wordsworth's letters testifies to the great impression the Chartreuse left upon the poet : "he used to talk so much of it to me."

In France

25 1 **when we chanced :** *i.e.* Wordsworth and Michel Beaupuy, an aristocratic altruist of fine purpose and intellect, who, in 1792 at Blois, tuned his young English friend's mind to sympathy with the Revolution. Beaupuy, general of a division, was killed in action in 1797.

25 9 **'Tis against that :** for individual angle of view, *cf.* note upon **22.**

Paris—September, 1792

26 — Professor Harper thinks that this description relates to an unknown and dangerous visit of Wordsworth's to Paris in 1793. If it relates to the known visit, the sequence of events would be as follows: On July 26 (1792), the Duke of Brunswick had issued, in the name of the allied princes, his threatening demand for the restoration to power of Louis XVI. The leaders of the people of Paris—Danton, Marat, and Robespierre—then used these threats as a goad to popular indignation. On August 9th, at night, the mob stormed the Tuileries, killed the guard, and held the King as hostage. On August 24th the Prussians entered Longwy, and news followed soon of the surrender of Verdun. In retaliation the extreme Jacobins then organized a wholesale massacre of royalist suspects in Paris ; from the 2nd to the 6th of September, many hundreds of men, women and children were butchered accordingly. The French troops, however, rallied unexpectedly at Valmy, September 20th, and the Republic was at once proclaimed. Wordsworth's mood, in reference to

> those September massacres,
> Divided from me by one little month

will now be clear.

26 13 **Saw them and touched**: it is characteristic of Wordsworth's mind to feel the ' presence of the past ' ; from line 9 to line 23 Wordsworth emphasises the truth of this sense, turning to analogies in support of his argument.

26 16 **The horse is taught his manage** : a reflection of a passage in Orlando's first speech in *As You Like It*. ' Manage '—paces, training.

27 25 **"sleep no more "** : *cf.* " Macbeth shall sleep no more " (*Macbeth*, Act II, Scene ii).

Bewildered Offering

27 11 **harsh necessity** : the 1805 version is more emphatic,

> Compelled by nothing else than absolute want
> Of funds for my support.

His heart was evidently not in the French cause to the point of starving for it ; but that is implied in the ensuing confession of his impotence to help.

27 19 **some who perished :** *i.e.* Girondist leaders put to death in October 1793.

28 24 **Friend :** as throughout, Coleridge.

28 25 **To thee unknown :** Wordsworth did not meet Coleridge until the autumn of 1795.

Grief at England's Hostility

28 7 **that delightful island :** *i.e.* Isle of Wight, where Wordsworth was staying in late summer, 1793, with William Calvert, brother of the Calvert who left Wordsworth £900 (Introduction, xvi). In a note (1842) preceding " Guilt and Sorrow," Wordsworth refers to the time, and there his reference to the fleet's preparation against France is milder.

Disillusionment

28 — A passage from the time of Wordsworth's hopeless search for refuge in Godwinism (*cf.* Introduction, xvi).

But Nature Abides

29 7 **wings that navigate cerulean skies :** an expression far from humble rusticity of diction (Introduction, xxii). Wordsworth readily mounts above ' neutral style ' in the inspired period of his life. In later years some of his attempts to do so fell into artificiality. Cerulean, stress on second syllable, comes from *Cœruleus*, for *cœluleus* (*cœlum*, sky) ' blue.'

29 16 The passage requires to be read thus : ' I, too, rejoiced before (the presence of) the winds . . . and (rejoiced) in lights and shades,' etc.

' Powers ' is in apposition to ' winds,' ' waters,' ' lights and shades.'

30 26 **how feeble have I been :** *cf.* in a larger sense, ' what man has made of man,' *Lines in Early Spring*, **40**.8.

If We have Eyes to See

30 — This passage is most significant. It shows the poet, restored by nature, grasping the belief that was to inspire his best work : nothing is common. The opening lines are almost in the spirit of *Acts*, x, 15, ' That which God hath cleansed, that call not thou common.' About this time there came to him also his sister's gentle guidance:

> She gave me eyes, she gave me ears;
> And humble cares, and delicate fears;
> A heart, the fountain of sweet tears;
> And love, and thought, and joy.
>
> (*The Sparrow's Nest*)

30 16-17 These two lines infer the spirit of divinity, a creative interrelation of nature and the human soul, that is the poet's highest aspiration. This is a difficult subject, but *cf.* Introduction, xxxiii-iv, and *Tintern Abbey*, **132.**105-7.

> of all the mighty world
> Of eye and ear,—both what they half create,
> And what perceive.

Snowdon

31 1-3 In one of those excursions . . . with a youthful friend: the friend was Robert Jones, the Cambridge companion with whom he had toured afoot on his first visit to France (*cf.* Introduction, xv, and **25.**44). Wordsworth and Calvert (*cf.* **28.**7, note) had parted after a carriage-accident. Wordsworth then walked, in late summer, 1793, over Salisbury Plain, visited Tintern Abbey (*cf.* **129.**1) and Goodrich Castle (*cf.* note 93), and made his way to Plas-yn-llan, North Wales, the home of Jones.

31 4 Bethgelert: some 5 miles south of Snowdon.

32 59-62 the roar of waters . . . felt by the starry heavens: again the susceptibility to this vague sound, here suffused to the extent of making, as it were, a sentient unity of all Nature (*cf.* **18.**20, *Tintern Abbey*, **129.**4, etc.).

33 67-68 The passage omitted here, contains development of this difficult thought which should be turned up by any reader philosophically interested. Particularly, there is a Platonic parallel where Wordsworth speaks of

> . . . a mind sustained
> By recognitions of transcendent power
> In sense conducting to ideal form . . .

(*cf.* also **89.**6 : ' The Form remains, the Function never dies ').

LYRICAL POEMS

My Heart Leaps Up

37 — Composed at a time of high creative activity, March, 1802. Coleridge had just paid a long-expected visit. *The Cuckoo* (p. 55) was written in the same week, and Dorothy Wordsworth records her brother's beginning at this same time an ode, almost certainly *Intimations of Immortality*.

37 7-9 These lines the poet placed as a heading to his Ode (*see* above).

37 9 **piety :** in the Latin sense, affection towards one's parents or native country ; here the faithful affection of a child of nature.

TO A SKYLARK

37 — Written at Rydal Mount in 1825. The thought is contained in *Prelude*, xiv, 382-86. This poem originally had three stanzas, the following being the second :

> To the last point of vision, and beyond,
> Mount, daring warbler !—that love-prompted strain,
> ('Twixt thee and thine a never-failing bond)
> Thrills not the less the bosom of the plain :
> Yet might'st thou seem, proud privilege ! to sing
> All independent of the leafy spring.

Wordsworth afterwards moved this stanza to *A Morning Exercise*. In the last line the bird seems to have a spirit that transcends its natural setting : (cf. *Cuckoo*, 55.15), a passage which, in Wordsworth's own words (*Preface* 1815), " dispossesses the creature almost of a corporeal existence " :

> No bird, but an invisible thing
> A voice, a mystery.

(cf. *Green Linnet*, **39**.39, " The voiceless Form he chose to feign ").

37 8 *Cf.* Shelley's *Skylark* :

> Like a poet hidden
> In the light of thought.

It should be noted that Wordsworth gives the wonder and rapture of the skylark's life, and yet retains connection with earth ; whereas Shelley ignores earthly relations, viewing the bird as a disembodied spirit.

THE GREEN LINNET

38 — Written in 1803 of the birds in the orchard at Dove Cottage, Grasmere. The first and last stanzas were changed considerably from the originals published in 1807. The last three lines of the first stanza then were :

> A whispering Leaf is now my joy,
> And then a bird will be the toy
> That doth my fancy tether.

and the first four of the last stanza were :

> While thus before my eyes he gleams,
> A Brother of the Leaves he seems ;
> When in a moment forth he teems
> His little song in gushes :

The *Edinburgh Review*—chiefly remembered by Wordsworthians for the beginning of Jeffrey's onslaught upon the *Excursion* : ' This will never do ! '—rightly objected to ' tether ' and ' teems,' and Wordsworth eventually accepted the criticism.

38 18 **Make all one band of paramours** : this word for ' lovers,' unexpected in reference to birds and flowers, gives a rich-proud tone to the line, above plain rusticity.

39 29-31 **flutter . . . sunny glimmerings** : Wordsworth's eyes seem to have been as quick and clear as those of the Japanese artists, famous for their drawings of birds in movement.

Impromptu

39 — Composed June 8, 1802. Omitted from several editions but republished, as Wordsworth says, ' at the request of a friend in whose presence the lines were thrown off." They concluded with the lines :

> Who would go "parading "
> In London, " and masquerading,"
> On such a night of June
> With that beautiful soft half-moon,
> And all these innocent blisses?
> On such a night as this is !

This less poetical ending may well be part of the playful warfare between Wordsworth and Lamb. The latter was often provocative about the advantages of London (*e.g.* in the famous letter, Jan. 30th, 1801).

LINES WRITTEN IN EARLY SPRING

40 — Published in *Lyrical Ballads*, 1798, " Actually composed," says Wordsworth, " while I was sitting by the side of the brook that runs down from the *Comb*, in which stands the village of Alford, through the grounds of Alfoxden. It was a chosen resort of mine."

40 4 sad thoughts : possibly resigned disillusionment over the cause of freedom in France (*cf.* Introduction, xxiii).

40 5 link : *cf.* Introduction, xxxi.

40 11 'tis my faith : the whole poem is representative of Wordsworth's creed in returning to the healing power of Nature.

TO A SKYLARK

41 — Written probably in 1801.

41 1-7 There is here fine freedom of rhythm, an ode-like beginning, which continues to l. 15, after which there is a falling-off. Wordsworth afterwards said, with preference for his 1825 *Skylark*, that he had only finished the earlier poem, with its ' respectably-tame conclusion,' because he liked the beginning so well.

The Withered Leaves

42 — Composed March 18, 1798, at Alfoxden.

EXPOSTULATION AND REPLY

43 — One of the *Lyrical Ballads* (1798) composed at Alfoxden.

43 15 Matthew : the figure of the old schoolmaster-friend is taken roughly from that of William Taylor, Wordsworth's schoolmaster at Hawkshead. ' Matthew ' also appears in *The Two April Mornings* and *The Fountain* ; but the reader is warned in one of the Fenwick Notes against too close an identification :

> This and other poems connected with Matthew would not gain by a literal detail of facts. Like the Wanderer in the *Excursion*, this

schoolmaster was made up of several, both of his class and of men of other occupations.

These 'Matthew poems' suffer occasionally from a matter-of-fact tone that Wordsworth is apt to adopt in his poems of ' neutral ' or un-exalted style, where any poetic license, such as inversion of normal order of words (*e.g.* ll. 10, 15 ; 44.6-7 ; 48.16, etc.), appears weaker by contrast with unassuming ease. But the ' Matthew ' poems have spontaneous movement and cheerful sanity—" a quaint gaiety of metre," as Pater calls it.

43 17 cannot choose but see : this doctrine of ' wise passiveness ' (l. 24 ; *cf.* also **52.17**, and Introduction, xxx) is very important in the study of Wordsworth, and it receives its clearest statement from here to l. 28.

THE TABLES TURNED

44 — Composed about the same time as the preceding poem, and published in *Lyrical Ballads*.

44 1 my Friend : it has been supposed that Hazlitt is the friend addressed.

45 21-22 One impulse . . . may teach : *i.e.* one moment prompting further inspiration or access of imaginative energy, fresher in power than any motive of analytical mood. This is the poet's strongest statement of his belief in inspiration from nature—Professor Herford thinks that Wordsworth had in mind at this moment his revolt from Godwinism.

45 26-28 Our meddling intellect . . . we murder to dissect : one of Wordsworth's extreme points of aversion from arrogance in scientific outlook.

THE TWO APRIL MORNINGS

45 — Written in 1799.

45 3 Matthew : *see* above, 43.15.

46 13 work : *i.e.* the project or excursion.

47 59 with a bough : originally ' with his bough.' Note how so slight a change can mean a turn from the familiarity of friendship to the objectivity of a painter.

THE FOUNTAIN

48 — Written in 1799.

48 4 **Matthew seventy-two**: *see* above, 43.15. The force of Wordsworth's warning against the subjection of art to biographical actuality is seen in the fact that William Taylor died in 1786, aged 32.

49 37-44 The passiveness of nature, akin to the desired poetic passiveness (*cf.* 43.24).

50 57 The young poet here speaks; from 48.21 to this point 'Matthew' was the speaker.

50 58-60 **complains . . . plains**: the identity of rhyme seems to have escaped Wordsworth's notice. What the French call 'rime riche' is for us no rhyme at all.

To the Nightingale

50 — Dated by Wordsworth 1806. Probably written at Coleorton, Leicestershire, the home of his friend Sir George Beaumont. No nightingales sing at Grasmere.

50 2 **"fiery heart"**: *cf.* 'and thus in May their hearts are set on fire,' l. 34 in Wordsworth's modernization of Chaucer, *The Cuckoo and the Nightingale.*

51 11 **Stock-dove**: Wordsworth probably meant the ringdove, or wood-pigeon.

51 20 **the song for me**: the gentler voice has often been quoted as characteristic of Wordsworth's own temperament, but this view is exaggerated by his later mildness; there are plenty of poems of stormier mood.

I Wandered Lonely as a Cloud

51 — Written in 1804 at Grasmere. The point of inspiration is clear from an account in Dorothy Wordsworth's Journal. The daffodils were in Gowbarrow Park, Ullswater, and they were seen on April 15th, 1802, by the poet and his sister, who wrote:

> I never saw daffodils so beautiful. They grew among the mossy stones, about and above them; some rested their heads upon these stones, as on a pillow for weariness; and the rest tossed and reeled and danced, and seemed as if they verily laughed with the wind that blew directly over the lake to them. They looked so gay, ever glancing. . . . There was here and there a little knot, and a few

stragglers higher up; but they were so few as not to disturb the simplicity, unity, and life of that one busy highway. We rested again and again. The bays were stormy, and we heard the waves at different distances, and in the middle of the water, like the sea.

This passage has become a *locus classicus* of comparison between the sensitive impressibility of Dorothy and the poetic imagination of her brother. The similarities are sufficiently striking. Dorothy, however, has a strong leaning towards sentiment, as appears in her pretty fancy of the weariness of the flowers' heads. It is a vulgar error to suppose Wordsworth sentimental. " His pathos," says Professor Raleigh, " is an unmitigated, hard pathos, beyond the reach of sentimental palliatives."

If Wordsworth imagines the budding twigs as sentient (cf. *Lines in Early Spring*, 40.16-20), or if he sees in a flower "thoughts that do often lie too deep for tears " (*see* end of *Immortality* Ode) that was because he felt to the depths of his being that the universe was pervaded with a Spirit of " joy in widest commonalty spread."

52 17 **I gazed—and gazed—but little thought:** another instance of ' wise passiveness ' (*cf.* 43.17).

52 20 **pensive mood:** *cf.* " from emotion recollected in tranquillity " (Introduction, xxiii).

52 21-22 These lines were contributed by Mrs Wordsworth.

52 24 **And dances with the daffodils:** thus, the climax of the poem is simple joy. There is neither plot nor moralizing.

To his Wife

52 — Written in 1824. Wordsworth married Mary Hutchinson on October 1802, having known her since childhood (cf. *She was a Phantom of Delight*, p. 63). The climax of the first stanza has a quaint brusqueness; the second has a plain tenderness akin to that of Cowper; and the climax of the third has a quickening of pulse that lifts it above homeliness.

WRITTEN IN MARCH

53 — ' While Resting on the Bridge at the Foot of Brother's Water ' is the rest of the full title. The poet says he wrote ' extempore.' The day was April 16th, 1802. The corresponding

entry in Dorothy Wordsworth's Journal is, if anything, closer than in the case of ' Daffodils,' but her brother had written his poem first in this case.

53 13-14 **fare ill . . . bare hill:** Wordsworth hardly ever plays with a rhyme like this. The effect is part of the Impromptu mood, however.

If This Great World

53 — Written in 1833.

53 3 **freedom, set, will rise again:** *cf.* 26.21, ' all things have second birth.'

53 5 **purblind crew:** Wordsworth was probably thinking of callous industrialists, under whose influence the people seemed to him so deteriorated that he opposed the Reform Bill (1832).

TO A BUTTERFLY

54 — Written in 1802, in the orchard, at ' Town-End,' Grasmere.

54 5 **not frozen seas more motionless ! :** it seems a far cry from a butterfly to a frozen sea ; but imagination has, with striking originality, abstracted the common attribute of stillness. The contrivance of such poetic abstraction is carefully noted by Wordsworth in a passage in the *Preface* of 1815 :

> These processes of imagination are carried on either by conferring additional properties upon an object, or abstracting from it some of those which it actually possesses, and thus enabling it to re-act upon the mind which hath performed the process, like a new existence.

TO MY SISTER

54 — Composed in front of Alfoxden House, spring 1798, and published in *Lyrical Ballads*. There are eight more stanzas, including the lines :

> One moment now may give us more
> Than years of toiling reason

which reiterate more bluntly the doctrine of ' one impulse from a vernal mood ' (45.21). These other stanzas contain some prosaic lines, equalled, I admit, by others in *We are Seven* and

The Sailor's Mother. Both those poems are included, however, for a special purpose, and I ventured to leave the eight stanzas out so that they should not disturb the lovely opening, compact in itself and so characteristic of Wordsworth's best mood.

54 3 from the tall larch : the break of rhythm, hanging an extra stress on ' sings,' has the look of a technique unconscious and inspired, especially if one considers that the poem was an impromptu sent by hand, by the little Basil Montagu, then Wordsworth's ward.

54 7-8 The scarcity and plainness of the adjectives should be noticed, and their order.

TO THE CUCKOO

55 — Written at Town-End, Grasmere, March 23-26, 1802. Some of the passages apparently most simple, limpid and direct, cost Wordsworth much thought. The second stanza, for instance, passed through many changes to reach final form forty years after its first conception. The second line was at one time ' Thy loud note smites my ear " ; it is interesting, in the light of **18.11-12**, to note Wordsworth's hankering after the striking expression ' shout ' which he restored. In example of the interest which can attach to changes of text, see Professor Dowden's Edition which gives them with such scholarly care as to provide food for an essay on this poem alone.

For similar effect cf. *The Cuckoo at Laverna, Sleep* (**79**.8), and *Impromptu* (**39**.8-9), also *Preface* 1815.

55 8 At once far off, and near : this description, apart from its fidelity to nature, could be applied philosophically as a natural analogy to Professor Whitehead's remark on Wordsworth's imagination : " He always grasps the whole of nature as involved in the tonality of the particular instance " (*cf.* note upon **16**).

55 15-16 *cf.* note upon **37**.

55 20 bush, and tree, and sky : again, classical economy and strength of selection (*cf.* **19**.24).

56 28 That golden time again : cf. *Intimations of Immortality*, l. 69, where the boy ' beholds the light, and whence it flows.' The cuckoo, this ' invisible thing,' becomes a bond of ' natural piety ' (**37**.9).

THE REVERIE OF POOR SUSAN

56 — Composed 1797. A poem drawing upon London memories.

56 1 **Wood Street**: off Cheapside in the City of London.

56 2 **Hangs**: originally ' there's '—note precision gained.

56 4 **In the silence of morning the song of the Bird**: perhaps an echo of *Ecclesiastes*, xii, 4, ' he shall rise up at the voice of the bird.'

56 7 **Lothbury**: another city street, near the Bank of England.

56 8 **a river flows on through the vale of Cheapside**: I cannot help thinking that this may have given Francis Thompson courage for ' Jacob's Ladder, Pitched betwixt Heaven and Charing Cross ' (in the poem beginning '' O world invisible, we view thee '').

56 9-12 Let us agree that this third stanza misses the strength of the rest.

56 16 **And the colours have all passed away from her eyes!**: note the ' hard, unmitigated pathos ' of the awakening from the daydream (*cf.* note **51**, on *Daffodils*), a characteristic ending that rings true. There was originally a last stanza referring to the ' outcast's ' home-coming. It was dropped, much to Lamb's satisfaction. If Wordsworth dwelt on plot he would engage a meaner attention and distract us from his main message of wonder over things in themselves.

THE SOLITARY REAPER

57 — Written between 1803 and 1805. Wordsworth had set out in August 1803 with his sister and Coleridge for a tour in Scotland. Dorothy notes in her Journal similar scenes and single workers: but the actual inspiration came from a MS. note by their friend Thomas Wilkinson upon his own experience:

> Passed a female who was reaping alone; she sung in Erse as she bended over her sickle; the sweetest human voice I ever heard; her strains were tenderly melancholy, and felt delicious, long after they were heard no more.

57 6 **melancholy strain**: *cf.* Wilkinson, above.

57 7-8 **Vale . . . overflowing with the sound**: this motif is frequent in Wordsworth, *cf.* ' cuckoo's sovereign cry Fills all the hollow of the sky ' (**39**.8-9).

57 11 **haunt**: correctly rhymed with ' chaunt.' The ' shady haunt among Arabian sands ' has an exotic note which, in a manner somewhat like that of Keats, rises to still richer music in the lines that follow.

57 15-16 $\begin{cases} \text{Breaking the silence of the seas} \\ \text{Among the farthest Hebrides.} \end{cases}$: Professor White-head makes this image his example in contrasting Wordsworth's mode of thought with that of Shelley. Whereas nature for Shelley changes and dissolves ' Like ghosts from an enchanter fleeing,' for Wordsworth " change is an incident which shoots across a background of endurance."

57 19 **old, unhappy, far-off things**: The Romantics turned to ' battles long ago ' mainly as a realm of colour to which to escape from an age of industrialism. Though at one time he contemplated a ' romantic ' epic, Wordsworth had little in common with this tendency. Had he followed such a theme in this instance, he would probably have dwelt on enduring human emotions and not on pageantry.

58 32 Wordsworth himself called attention to his adoption of Wilkinson's words as they stood (*see* above).

AT THE GRAVE OF BURNS

58 — Probably written about the time of the Scottish tour. On August 18, 1803, the Wordsworths with Coleridge visited the grave in Dumfries. Wordsworth always held his brother poet in generous veneration. Obviously they had in common their sympathy with lowly characters, and Wordsworth wished humbly and sincerely that they had met. The travellers were deeply moved by thoughts of Burns's divine fire and human unhappiness, and called to mind his *Bard's Epitaph*, the stanza-form of which, Burns's favourite, Wordsworth here adopts.

58 19 **the flower, whose modest worth**: *i.e.* " Wee modest crimson-tipped flow'r," Burns's *Mountain Daisy*.

58 20 " **glinted** " **forth**: quoted from the same poem, l. 15.

59 39 **Criffel**: *i.e.* Crowfell, a mountain in Kirkcudbright, 1800 ft. Visibility from Skiddaw gives sense of ' neighbours.'

60 50 " **poor Inhabitant below** " : quoted from Burns's *Bard's Epitaph*, l. 19.

60 62 **the Stripling died**: Burns's son, Wallace.

60 78 **For which it prayed :** *i.e.* in *To Ruin*, " when shall my soul, in silent peace, Resign life's joyless day ? "

STEPPING WESTWARD

61 — Dorothy Wordsworth, the ' Fellow-traveller ' of Wordsworth's note, describes the scene more amply as on Sunday, September 11, 1803, and adds that her brother wrote the poem ' long after.' The note explains the circumstances. Most characteristic of Wordsworth are the lines

> 'twas a sound
> Of something without place or bound.

The greeting thus appears like a note in natural harmony sounded by the spirit of the place.

LINES

62 — Written in 1806. Charles James Fox, the famous Whig, died on September 13, 1806. He was a great leader of opposition, approving of the French Revolution, and fighting all forms of abuse and tyranny. Wordsworth held him in honour and had sent him, some years earlier, with earnest deference, a copy of the *Lyrical Ballads*.

62 3 **unison of streams :** for this sound *cf.* 18.20 ; and also 15.6, for the imaginative associations of storms.

62 11 **Comforter :** in meaning probably not more definite than ' spirit of comfort.'

62 13 **many thousands now are sad :** only a few days before his death Fox had brought in a measure to abolish the slave trade.

She was a Phantom of Delight

63 — Written in 1804 at Town-End. In this poem Wordsworth gives three aspects of his maturing love for Mary Hutchinson, his wife.

64 22 **pulse of the machine :** this strange phrase is referred by Professor Dowden to Hamlet's signature, to Ophelia, " Thine . . . whilst this machine is to him," and with stronger conviction to a book, Bartram's *Travels*, with which Wordsworth was familiar, where ' *machine* ' indicates the whole organism of life, moving as the " *pulse* of nature " wakes.

A COMPLAINT

64 — Written at Town-End, 1806. It is usually supposed that Coleridge is addressed in this poem, which seems to me, however, to have the strong feeling of one of those moving fictions that Wordsworth wrought upon some impulse from memory ; a vein in which the ' Lucy ' poems (pp. 68-70) are examples more beautiful still.

THE AFFLICTION OF MARGARET

65 — Probably written a few years before 1804, the date given from memory by Wordsworth, who adds that the poem is based on the actual case of a poor widow who would go out from her shop in Penrith to ask strangers about her lost son. Wordsworth's calm and serious pathos rises to a climax in stanza viii that is superb beyond a poor woman's vocabulary (' incommunicable,' l. 56, is a word used of sleep to intensify the remoteness of death) ; but stanza x with its plain, passionate nature-images is still more grand.

Glad Sight

68 — Written probably about 1845. The gentle moralising in the poem does not hinder the serene, quick beauty which the aged poet had at his command.

Strange Fits of Passion have I known

68 — Written in Germany, early in 1799. This poem and the three poems that follow refer to a ' Lucy ' of whom nothing is known. Possibly ' Lucy ' is an entirely imaginary person : it seems more probable that she is based upon an early memory wrought with creative imagination to the figure of these beautiful poems. There is in them, says Mr Read, a " passion that is too strong to be merely visionary and too idealistic to be associated with mundane emotions." Professor Harper supposes an actual love affair, and suggests the scene of it.

I travelled among Unknown Men

69 — 1799. *See* note above, on ' Lucy ' poems.

69 1 **unknown men :** these plain words, of classic reticence, are more powerful to convey nostalgia than any particularised attempt at poignancy.

69 13 mornings showed . . . nights concealed : imagination heightened by love transcends distance, day and night.

She Dwelt among the Untrodden Ways

70 — Germany, 1799. *See* note 68 on ' Lucy ' poems.
70 2 springs of Dove : the Dove rises near Buxton.

A Slumber did my Spirit seal

70 — Germany, 1799. See note 68 on ' Lucy ' poems. An editor feels bound to point out the sombre richness of ' diurnal ' and the stern severity of selection in the last line : but the poem is really beyond comment.

SONNETS

Wordsworth was a most prolific writer of sonnets. There are no less than 516 in his published work. Many were written in later years without ardent feeling, but those that bear his true inspiration are masterly in revelation of his spirit, and their noble success had untold influence in restoring the sonnet in English Poetry.

In form Wordsworth's sonnets vary. Usually his *octave* keeps the Italian rhyming pattern (a b b a, a b b a) but his *sestet* varies a good deal, as will be clear at once from the fact that of the first seven sonnets in the present *Selections* only two have the same order of rhymes in the last six lines. There are, in the 33 sonnets included, 14 variations of *sestet*. Nearly a third of these sonnets have three rhymes in the *octave*, instead of two ; and rather more than a third have an over-running of sense, without break or pause, from the octave to the sestet (e.g. *England*, No. III, p. 74 ; *Mutability*, p. 78). In this last characteristic Wordsworth followed Milton. Indeed it was the example of Milton that drew him to the sonnet in the first place.

" In the cottage of Town-End, one afternoon in 1801," he told Miss Fenwick, " my sister read to me the sonnets of Milton. I had long been well acquainted with them, but I was particularly struck on that occasion with the dignified simplicity and majestic harmony that runs through most of them—in character so totally different from the Italian and still more so from Shakespeare's fine sonnets. I took fire, if I may be allowed to say so, and produced three sonnets the same afternoon—the first I ever wrote, except an irregular one at school."—(*Grosart*, Vol. III).

Of those three sonnets, Wordsworth only remembered " I grieved for Buonaparte," the date of which is, however, 1802— a correction confirmed by Dorothy's entry in her Journal.

Nuns fret not

72 — Date uncertain. Published 1807. The tone of gentle apology is probably due to a hard-dying feeling that the trammel of conventional form laid a secondary, unworthy condition on poetic impulse—was still, in fact, something of a ' trade in classic niceties ' (cf. *Prelude*, vi, 109). Wordsworth had now come, however, to accept limitation or restraint as a possible blessing (*cf*. l. 13) ; this is the dominating thought in the *Ode to Duty* which appeared at the same time.

72 3 students . . . pensive citadels : *cf.* Milton in *Il Penseroso* :

> Or let my lamp at midnight hour,
> Be seen in some high lonely tower.

72 6 Furness-fells : hills between Windermere and the River Duddon.

England, 1802

73-74 — The events leading up to the Treaty of Amiens (March 1802) were as follows: from 1793 to 1797 the First Coalition of Powers against France had been beaten on land. Holland and Spain joined France, and Napoleon made successful treaties with Prussia and Austria. England was saved by her Fleet, but now stood alone. With the English and French peoples weary of war, the Treaty came as ' a peace which all men are glad of, but no man could be proud of.' It left France mistress of Holland, Belgium, Switzerland and Italy, and of the left bank of the Rhine. Never had she appeared more powerful ; and henceforth, from the renewal of war, in May 1803, Napoleon's whole career was directed against England.

At the first safe opportunity, after the Treaty, Wordsworth went with his sister to meet Annette Vallon and the child

Caroline, at Calais. It was a meeting of amicable understanding ; the passage of years had evidently dimmed the former love-affair (*cf.* Introduction, xv) beyond recall. The Wordsworths returned after a month, landing at Dover, August 30.

" The next day was very hot," writes Dorothy, adding that they bathed and " sate upon Dover Cliffs, and looked upon France with many a melancholy and tender thought."

74 (II) A famous sonnet, but not very clear. The poet ' shrunk ' at the inviting calm of the Channel ' barrier ' and felt the importance of keeping it inviolate. Yet protection will be forthcoming for virtue. The elements, in themselves nothing, become divine power under the Almighty's decree, which from man demands greatness of soul as a condition of freedom. (*Cf. Prelude*, **29.**14-26 ; and, for spiritual faith, *Ode to Duty*, **136.**47-8.)

74 (III) Wordsworth tells us that the sonnet expresses the shock with which, on his return to London (September), he saw the contrast between the ' vanity and parade of our own country ' and the quiet desolation in France. The same spirit prompts the grander outburst of No. IV.

74 (III) 1 **Friend :** Coleridge.

75 (IV) 14 **herself :** ' heart ' is treated as ' soul,' for which Wordsworth uses the feminine pronoun.

76 (VI) 4 **pomp of waters :** Professor Dowden notes the quotation as from Daniel, *Civil War*, Book II, Stanza 7.

NOVEMBER, 1806

76 2 **mighty Empire overthrown :** *i.e.* Prussia. After the battle of Jena (October 14) Napoleon occupied Berlin (October 25). On November 20 he declared a blockade against England.

COMPOSED UPON WESTMINSTER BRIDGE, SEPTEMBER 3, 1802

77 — This lovely sonnet was composed on the outward journey (*cf.* note on *England*, 1802, above). It actually may have been finished on the coach-top. The poet more than once, with his sister, held considerable passages in memory until they could be written down (e.g. *Tintern Abbey. Cf.* note p. 189). September 3rd is the poet's error, corrected in a note to Miss Fenwick. They had taken the Dover coach early in the morning of July 31st. Dorothy writes :

The city, St Paul's, with the river, and a multitude of little boats, made a most beautiful sight as we crossed Westminster Bridge. The houses were not overhung by their cloud of smoke, and they were spread out endlessly, yet the sun shone so brightly, with such a fierce light, that there was even something like the purity of one of nature's own grand spectacles.

INSIDE OF KING'S COLLEGE CHAPEL, CAMBRIDGE

77 — Possibly written in the winter of 1820, when Wordsworth visited his brother, Master of Trinity.

77 1 **royal Saint :** Henry VI, founder of Eton and King's.

The World

78 — Date uncertain. Published in 1807.

78 4 **boon :** originally ' boon ' meant prayer, but it gathered a secondary meaning, ' gift.'

78 9-10 **I'd rather be a Pagan :** a fearless challenge to lethargy.

78 14 **Triton :** a reflection of Spenser's ' Triton blowing loud his wreathed horne ' in ' *Colin Clout*,' l. 245. ' Proteus ' occurs three lines later.

MUTABILITY

78 — Written about 1821, one of the " Ecclesiastical Sonnets."

78 13-14 The climax of this sonnet combines force with delicacy, in a style reached by very few poets.

A Godhead

79 — Written 1908.

79 3-4 **like the universal Pan ; But more exalted :** the animating principle above the pagan spirit of life-in-nature, might be taken for a rough representation of Wordsworth's theology,— apart from his later orthodoxy.

79 10 **the arduous strife :** *cf.* ' terrors, pains ' in *A Dark Inscrutable Workmanship* (p. 6).

TO SLEEP

79 — Date uncertain. Published 1807.

The sonnet has selection of lovely images as its natural purpose (*e.g.* l. 4). It is a pity to piece them out.

ON THE EXTINCTION OF THE VENETIAN REPUBLIC

80 — Written in 1802. Venice had not joined against France but had refused to recognise the Republic. When in 1796 the Council tried to negotiate with Buonaparte, it was too late. By the Treaty of Campo Formio (October 1797) Napoleon handed over Venice to Austria.

80 1 east in fee : until the latter half of the fifteenth century Venice dominated the Near East, having reduced Tyre, Trieste, and Constantinople. She grew in sea-power, in territory, and in riches accruing from eastern trade and from transport during the Crusades.

' Fee ' here has the old legal meaning ' absolute ownership.' The word originally meant ' cattle ' (A.S. *feoh* ; Mod. G. *Vieh*. *Cf*. Lat. *pecus*, whence ' pecuniary '), and it gave ' fief,' ' feudal,' etc.

80 8 espouse the . . . Sea : a reference to the historic Ascension Day ceremony in which the Doge threw a wedding pledge to the Adriatic.

80 10 strength decay : in strife with the Turks, who took Constantinople in 1453.

TO TOUSSAINT L'OUVERTURE

80 — Written in 1802. Toussaint was born a slave and joined in the negro revolt for liberation of Hayti, 1791. The French made him chief of the army of St Domingo for services against the Spanish (a breach made in their defences earned him the name L'Ouverture) ; but when Napoleon re-established slavery Toussaint refused to obey. An expedition was sent against him. When he submitted he was treacherously arrested and thrown into a French dungeon where, after ten months, he died, April 1803.

MARY QUEEN OF SCOTS

81 — One of the " Poems composed or suggested during a tour, in the summer of 1833 " to Oban, Staffa and Iona. Mary, held prisoner in 1567, following upon the murder of Darnley, escaped from Lochleven, and, after the battle of Langside, crossed to Workington in a fishing-boat, May 16th, 1568.

81 5 **Star:** the frequency of the lonely star image in Wordsworth will be noted (*cf.* **75.** iv, 9 ; **10.**26 ; **92.**9).

81 9 **Saturnian:** the Roman Saturn is usually identified with the Greek Kronos—the aged figure with the scythe—though they had little in common except antiquity.

81 14 **Fotheringay:** at which castle Mary was beheaded, February 8, 1587.

TO LADY FITZGERALD, IN HER SEVENTIETH YEAR

81 — Written probably in 1824. Lady Fitzgerald had been described to Wordsworth by their friend Lady Beaumont.

81 11 **toward:** Wordsworth had previously regarded this word as disyllabic.

PERSONAL TALK

82 — Date uncertain. Published, 1807. These sonnets have something of the traits of wistfulness and of sensuous delicacy which we find in Keats's gentler work.

82 (I) Wordsworth says that one line in this sonnet almost cost them the friendship of Miss Fenwick, who " stigmatized one line of it as vulgar, and worthy only of having been composed by a country squire." Wordsworth adds that the reader is left to guess which.

82 (I) 8 **floors:** *i.e.* dancing-floors.

82 (II) 13 **Lady . . . Moor:** Desdemona and Othello.

82 (II) 14 **Una:** from Spenser's *Faerie Queene*, Book I.

83 (III) 9-12 These lines are inscribed under Wordsworth's statue in Westminster Abbey.

Twilight

83 — Date uncertain. Published, 1815.

It is a Beauteous Evening

84 — Composed " on the beach near Calais," August 1802.

84 9 **Dear Child:** Caroline (*cf.* note on *England*, 1802, above). The thought of innocence intimately directed by nature should be compared with the *Ode to Duty:*

> Glad Hearts ! without reproach or blot ;
> Who do thy work and know it not :— (135.13-14).

84　14 This last line is reminiscent of *Genesis*, xxviii, 16 : " Surely the Lord is in this place ; and I knew it not."

Speak !

84 — Composed about 1832. The poet tells how the inspiration for this sonnet came during a walk with his daughter Dora :

> In the month of January when Dora and I were walking from Town-End, Grasmere, across the vale, snow being on the ground, she espied in the thick though leafless hedge a bird's-nest half-filled with snow. Out of this comfortless appearance arose this Sonnet, which was in fact, written without the least reference to any individual object, but merely to prove to myself that I could, if I thought fit, write in a strain that poets have been fond of.

Most Grievous Loss

85 — The sonnet, says Wordsworth, " was in fact suggested by my daughter Catherine long after her death." Catherine was nearly four when she died, June 1812. The sonnet was published in 1815.

BETWEEN NAMUR AND LIEGE

85 — One of the " Memorials of a Tour on the Continent, 1820."

The Moon

86 — Composed 1846.

THE TROSSACHS

87 — One of the poems of a tour in Scotland, 1831.

87　3 his autumn gone : the sad vein in the beginning of the sonnet is prompted by thought of Scott, who had gone away to Italy, broken in health. He died in September, 1832.

COMPOSED BY THE SIDE OF GRASMERE LAKE

87 — Written in 1807. Wordsworth had returned to his home from Coleorton, Sir George Beaumont's place in Leicestershire.

SEPTEMBER 1815

88 — Composed December 1815. Wordsworth expressed regret that his joys ''mid frost and snow' (l. 13) should offend, by contrast, people of less robust health.

JOURNEY RENEWED

88 — No. 28 of *The River Duddon* Sonnets, which were composed between 1806 and 1820.

AFTER-THOUGHT

89 — The last of the *Duddon* series (*cf.* 88, above). In the moving image of the river the poet sees as it were a dissolution of the limits of time, so that apprehension over personal fates is vain.

89 6 **Form . . . Function never dies:** the ideal is permanent though the personal must fade.

89 7 The poet referred this line to classical origin; *i.e.* Bion, *Lament*, l. 103 (quoted by Dowden).

89 14 Wordsworth also drew attention to *Paradise Lost*, Book VIII, l. 282, where Adam wishes to know the Maker:

> From whom I have that thus I move and live
> And feel that I am happier than I know.

NARRATIVE AND REFLECTIVE POEMS

" If thou indeed"

92 — Date uncertain. Published in 1827.

"These verses," says Wordsworth, in a Fenwick note, "were written some time after we had become resident at Rydal Mount; and I will take occasion from them to observe upon the beauty of that situation, as being backed and flanked by lofty fells, which bring the heavenly bodies to touch, as it were, the earth upon the mountain tops, while the prospect in front lies open to a length of level valley, the extended lake, and a terminating ridge of low hills; so that it gives an opportunity to the inhabitants of the place of noticing the stars in both the positions here alluded to, namely, on the tops of the mountains, and as winter-lamps at a distance among the leafless trees."

WE ARE SEVEN

93 — Composed in 1798 at Alfoxden. Published in *Lyrical Ballads*. Wordsworth actually met the little girl, here described, at Goodrich Castle during his first visit to the Wye (1793). The theme, of a child's incapacity to conceive of death, is announced in a first stanza which was added after completion of the rest. Professor Bradley repudiates the announcement as inadequate because it attributes the child's inner conviction to animal health and not to childhood's holding, as Wordsworth elsewhere says, ' an intimation or assurance . . . that some part of our nature is imperishable '—which belief links the plain little poem to the great *Immortality* Ode.

This first stanza was actually thrown off by Coleridge to meet his friend's desire for some such preface, and its first line originally read :

> A little child, dear brother Jem.

Wordsworth afterwards removed this playful allusion to their friend James Tobin and, with the fine discrimination of genius, turned the ridiculous to the sublime by leaving simply beats of silence.

(Mr de la Mare expressed to me some years ago his admiration of that silence ; and I have heard Mr Drinkwater, characteristic-ally enough, praise the proud tone of language noted under **38.17-18**.)

The poem is characteristic of Wordsworth's attitude to chil-dren : he does not see life with their eyes, but he is full of earnest wonder at their view, and so there is a real and steady humility in his persistent questioning.

LUCY GRAY

95 — Written in 1799 at Goslar. Wordsworth founded the poem on an actual incident of a little girl similarly lost in a snow-storm and drowned. His poetical aim he describes as " contrasting the imaginative influences, which I have endeavoured to throw over common life with Crabbe's matter-of-fact style of handling subjects of the same kind."

Wordsworth adds that he does this not in disparagement but to encourage ' catholic judgment.'

96 18-20 Wordsworth felt that ' no town or village girl ' would notice the moon by day, and that this trait gives thus a greater sense of solitude.

97 56 **And further there were none :** after this point Wordsworth departs from the original story, in which the child's body was recovered. This turn towards the unknown lifts the tale to phantom beauty.

THE SAILOR'S MOTHER

98 — Composed 1802. Wordsworth's memory gives date 1800, and he adds, to Miss Fenwick:

> I met this woman near the Wishing-Gate, on the high-road that then led from Grasmere to Ambleside. Her appearance was exactly as here described, and such was her account, nearly to the letter.

Most editors omit this poem from ' selections,' apparently thinking it too uncompromisingly bare. I include it because it is characteristically uncompromising, leaves off without moral or comment, and achieves the effect of a ' genre ' picture.

HART-LEAP WELL

99 — Composed early in 1800. Wordsworth prefixes the following note :

> Hart-Leap Well is a small spring of water, about five miles from Richmond in Yorkshire, and near the side of the road that leads from Richmond to Askrigg. Its name is derived from a remarkable Chase, the memory of which is preserved by the monuments spoken of in the second Part of the following Poem, which monuments do now exist as I have there described them.

99 1 **Wensley Moor :** in Yorkshire, N. Riding.

99 2 **motion of a summer's cloud :** this simile was intimately natural to Wordsworth's mind, cf. *I wandered lonely as a cloud.*

99 11-12 The contrast offered in these two lines should be noted. Other contrasts will be found skilfully supporting the main motif of the piece.

99 19 Blanch, Swift and Music: fine names for hounds, *cf.* John Peel's ' Bellman and True ' etc., north-country names. A dog at Mary Hutchinson's home was named ' Music.'

100 21 cheered and chid: *i.e.* encouraged and scolded alternately.

100 39 yeaned: born, brought forth (*cf.* A.S. *eanian*, from past part. of *eacan*, to increase).

101 75-76 Swale ... Ure: two Yorkshire rivers that join to make the Yorkshire Ouse.

102 97 The moving accident is not my trade: a conscious contrast between his own gifts and those which Coleridge had put forth in *The Ancient Mariner*.

103 101 Hawes ... Richmond: Yorkshire towns.

104 145-56 These three stanzas afford good example of Wordsworth's capacity for pathos without sentimentality.

105 177-80 The plain statement of a moral, possibly obtrusive in a lyric, comes in here as a quiet after-thought, rounding off a long poem.

RESOLUTION AND INDEPENDENCE

106 — Written in 1802. " Probably, if we must choose," says Professor Bradley, " the most Wordsworthian of Wordsworth's poems, and the best test of ability to understand him." Dorothy Wordsworth's Journal throws a good deal of light on the composition. She and her brother had met the old Leech-gatherer near Dove Cottage, their first Grasmere home, in September 1800. She refers to him as " almost double " (*cf.* **108**.66) and as having an interesting face and dark eyes (*cf.* **109**.91). He was of Scotch parents (*cf.* **109**.97). " His trade was to gather leeches, but now leeches were scarce " (*cf.* **110**.124-26).

" The account of him," says Wordsworth himself, " is taken from his own mouth. I was in the state of feeling described in the beginning of the poem, while crossing over Barton Fell. . . . The image of the hare I then observed on the ridge of the Fell." Thus the poet places the encounter on the lonely moors, the proper setting for the old man's work and for the eerie sense of solitude which kindles the poet's wonder and stirs his resolution. " A person reading the poem with feelings like mine," says

Wordsworth (Letter, 14, vi. 1802) " will have been awed and controlled, expecting something spiritual or supernatural." Wordsworth was probably anxious as to his slender means of livelihood. A visit from his brother John, persevering in his career as a ship's officer, had induced in Wordsworth self-reproach over his own comparative idleness (*cf.* stanza vi) ; and he takes to himself the example of the old Leech-gatherer's fortitude with all the earnestness of his ardent imagination.

106 5 **Stock-dove :** *i.e.* wood-pigeon (*cf.* 51.11).

107 28 **blind thoughts :** *cf.* ' a trouble to my dreams ' (8.44) ; ' blank misgivings ' (142.148) ; ' all troubled me ' (111.128).

107 36 *See* end of note above, on this poem in general.

107 43 **Chatterton, the marvellous Boy :** Thomas Chatterton, born 1752, was the boy who for a time successfully issued forged mediæval manuscripts, and then, after the misery of a sordid struggle for livelihood, embittered by disappointment, poisoned himself at the age of eighteen, author of much work including poetry of high imaginative power.

107 44 **in his pride :** contradicts (75.iv, 14) where the Soul is referred to as ' her '; but ' Soul' here stands for ' Boy.'

107 45 **Him who walked :** *i.e.* Burns. For the thought, *cf.* 58.19-30.

108 (VIII) After the eighth stanza came originally the following, which Wordsworth omitted in later editions because Coleridge censured it in *Biographia Literaria* :

> My course I stopped as soon as I espied
> The Old Man in this naked wilderness :
> Close by a Pond, upon the further side,
> He stood alone : a minute's space I guess
> I watch'd him, he continuing motionless :
> To the Pool's further margin then I drew ;
> He being all the while before me in full view.

Professor Raleigh, admitting the ' matter-of-factness ' which Coleridge blamed, defends the stanza thus :

> But has it no poetic value here? Is it not spoken exactly as a witness would speak who is about to tell how he saw a murder done or a life saved ? Does it not prepare the reader for great doings? And, finally, is he disappointed ?

108 61 seems a thing endued with sense : contemplation imaginatively animates even a boulder.

109 XII and XIII The inversions, ' he the pond' etc. (*cf.* ll. 79, 82, 83, 85, 86, 87), and the use of auxiliary ' did,' are curiously frequent here ; but the awkwardness is powerless to hinder the steady grandeur of the whole conception.

110 107 Wordsworth's sense of wonder here approaches a state of trance.

110 119 The poet falls to questioning again somewhat as in *We are Seven*, but with more passion and less obstinacy.

111 128 all troubled me : ' Trouble ' frequently means, in Wordsworth, ' imaginative stir ' (*cf.* **107**.28).

TO THE REV. DR WORDSWORTH

111 — Composed Christmastide 1819 and published 1820, addressing the *River Duddon* Sonnets to the poet's brother Christopher, then Rector of Lambeth (*cf.* l. 65). Some stanzas have a loving local colour like passages in Hardy's *Under the Greenwood Tree* (*e.g.* **111**.11-12), linked always, however, with Wordsworth's ' natural piety ' (*e.g.* **112**.28-30).

111 3 The force of ' smitten,' used of moonlight, should be noticed.

113 51 Cytherea's zone : the girdle of Venus, who was said to have sprung from sea-foam near Cythera. Her girdle was wrought with figures of love. The ' Thunderer ' in the next line is, of course, Jove.

113 65 Lambeth : *see* first note on this poem.

" BLEAK SEASON WAS IT, TURBULENT AND WILD "

114 — Probably composed in 1800. Not published until 1851. The poem is an extract originally quoted by Bishop Wordsworth, the poet's nephew and first editor, from *The Recluse*, Book I, Part I, *Home at Grasmere*, not included in the *Works*. The description applies to Wordsworth's journey (December, 1799) from Sockburn, County Durham, to Grasmere, with his sister. They had the Hutchinsons' horses as far as Wensley Dale, then walked on, by frozen roads through Askrigg, Sedbergh and Kendal, in wind and snow.

114 6 **Wensley's rich vale** : the valley of the River Ure, N. Riding.

114 6 **Sedbergh** : about 12 miles east of Kendal.

Chronicles of the Vale

115 — An excerpt from *The Brothers* (1800). ' The homely Priest of Ennerdale' is the speaker, and he is addressing a visitor.

> 'Twas one well known to him in former days,
> A Shepherd-lad ; who ere his sixteenth year
> Had left that calling, tempted to entrust
> His expectations to the fickle winds
> And perilous waters ; with the mariners
> A fellow-mariner ; and so had fared
> Through twenty seasons ; but he had been reared
> Among the mountains, and he in his heart
> Was half a shepherd on the stormy seas.

He returns to find his brother dead years before. In the last two lines of the passage quoted above, Wordsworth may well have been thinking of his brother John, who shared his love of their native mountains.

Nature's Door

116 — These lines are taken from *Devotional Incitements*, written in 1832. The present section of the poem is ushered in with the lines :

> Alas ! the sanctities combined
> By art to unsensualize the mind,
> Decay and languish ; or, as creeds
> And humours change, are spurned like weeds :

The whole passage speaks of the blessings of nature ; but though the doctrine may be akin to Rousseauism, the application and mode of it are different, first because Wordsworth's ' scattered poor' are admired figures of the dales, and secondly because Wordsworth establishes (from line 19 onwards) a tone of conservative piety.

A Grasmere Shepherd

117 — This fragment from *Michael* (1800) should be compared with similar work in the *Prelude* (*e.g.* pp. 23 to 25). The story of

Michael is one of an old man forced by adversity to send his one
lad out into the world. As a parting pledge they lay the first
stones of a sheep-fold together. With characteristic brevity
Wordsworth passes over news of the absent son's downfall,
and the noble old shepherd is left disconsolate.

> And to that hollow dell from time to time
> Did he repair, to build the Fold of which
> His flock had need. 'Tis not forgotten yet
> The pity which was then in every heart
> For the Old Man—and 'tis believed by all
> That many and many a day he thither went,
> And never lifted up a single stone.

ANIMAL TRANQUILLITY AND DECAY

118 — Written in 1798 and published in *Lyrical Ballads*. The
passage is kin with another fragment called *The Old Cumberland
Beggar*, and was possibly conceived originally as part of it. The
presentation of the aged figure, merged into his natural surround-
ings, is characteristic of Wordsworth.

THE SMALL CELANDINE

119 — Written in 1804. A premonition of old age, and
eventually placed by the poet in poems referring to that period.
119 13 with inly-muttered voice : this is to be taken literally
as one of Wordsworth's eccentricities.

The Mountain Daisy

120 — This reflective poem, in ' triplets,' an unusual form,
is included to show that the aged poet had moments of gentle
but beautiful inspiration. He was 74 when he wrote this.

NUTTING

121 — Written in 1799 for the *Prelude*. Wordsworth said
that the verses arose out of the remembrance of feelings he had
often had, when a boy, in the woods between Esthwaite and
Graythwaite. For spiritual refining of animal nature, the

passage should be compared with *Night-Snares* (5.17-25) ; *The Palfreys* (14.38-40), etc.

121 5 cottage-threshold : *i.e.* Dame Tyson's, *cf.* **11.**10.

121 11 Dame : *cf.* **121.**5, above.

122 54 Maiden : Dorothy Wordsworth.

A NIGHT-PIECE

122 — Composed in January 1798, on the road near Nether Stowey—Wordsworth says ' extempore.' The entry in his sister's diary is close to the poem in main features :

> The sky spread over with one continuous cloud, whitened by the light of the moon, which, though her dim shape was seen, did not throw forth so strong a light as to chequer the earth with shadows. At once the clouds seemed to cleave asunder, and left her in the centre of a black-blue vault. She sailed along, followed by multitudes of stars, small, and bright, and sharp ; their brightness seemed concentrated.

THE SIMPLON PASS

123 — Published separately (1845) but actually part of the *Prelude*, Bk. VI, 1804, in which year it was probably written, though Wordsworth gave the date 1799.

123 3 did we journey : *i.e.* Wordsworth and Jones, who crossed the Alps together in the summer of 1790 (*cf.* Introduction, xv). On their return they bought a boat in Basle and floated down to Cologne.

123 6 stationary blasts of waterfalls : the phrase owes something of its force to the process described under **54.**5 (note, p. 166).

124 11 crags that spake : *cf.* **15.**7-8.

> Beneath some rock, listening to notes that are
> The ghostly language of the ancient earth

124 18 Characters of the great Apocalypse : *i.e.* the writings traced by Nature's hand in revelation of her mystery.

Fragment from "The Recluse"

124 — For *The Recluse*, see note on p. 147 dealing with the history of the *Prelude*. What was finished of *The Recluse* was published by Bishop Wordsworth, the poet's nephew and first

biographer, in his *Memoirs* ; but the conclusion of Book I was
offered by Wordsworth ' as a kind of Prospectus ' in the Preface
to the *Excursion* (1814), from which the present lines are taken.
That the style is Miltonic will be seen not only from Milton's
phrases such as " Numerous Verse " and the quotation, l. 23,
from *Paradise Lost* (vii 31), but from the whole lofty tone of
solemn dedication to the poetic task.

124 11-12 **Whether from breath of outward circumstance, Or
from the Soul :** the old philosophical difficulty of origin of creative
impulse (*cf.* note on **30.**16-17) is brushed aside in the grand
aspiration of the lines following.

125 24-27 **Beauty . . . surpassing . . . earth's materials :** we
are reminded of Plato's notion of absolute Beauty (*Symposium*)—
cf. Introduction, xxxvi.

125 30 Homer refers to Elysian fields as a blissful abode at
the world's end, near Oceanus. In later poetry blessed heroes
were said to inhabit ' Fortunate Isles.'

125 31 **Sought in the Atlantic :** a reference to Plato's imagined
isle, Atlantis. Most characteristic is it of Wordsworth to find
the things of classical ' paradise ' ' a simple produce of the
common day ' (l. 37).

ELEGIAC STANZAS

SUGGESTED BY A PICTURE OF PEELE CASTLE

126 — When I let my selection end with the seventh stanza,
I did not perceive the danger, to which Professor Raleigh calls
attention, that over-concentration on lines 15-16, without the
further context, may foster the popular error which supposes
poetry to partake essentially of untrue romance. Nothing is
further from Wordsworth's intent.   In the line

> The light that never was, on sea or land,

the first comma indicates clearly that the longing is for the ideal
(*cf.* **125.**24-27 above) and not for any glamorous earthly effect.
Stanzas 8 and 9 at once make this trebly clear :

> Such, in the fond illusion of my heart,
> Such Picture would I at that time have made :
> And seen the soul of truth in every part,
> A steadfast peace that might not be betrayed.

> So once it would have been,—'tis so no more;
> I have submitted to a new control:
> A power is gone, which nothing can restore;
> A deep distress hath humanised my soul.

The ' deep distress ' was grief over the death of his brother John, lost at sea, Feb. 5th, 1805.

126 1 **thy neighbour once:** *i.e.* during a Cambridge vacation when staying with a relative at the village of Rampside. The ' Peele Castle ' described is south of Barrow-in-Furness.

126 8 **It trembled, but it never passed away:** for ' back-ground of endurance ' *cf*. note 57.15.

A POET'S EPITAPH

127 — Composed 1799 in Germany.

127 1 **Statist:** statesman.

127 11 **Doctor:** a divine such as Wordsworth scorns in the *Prelude*. He would see that he had a comfortable cushion to kneel on.

127 18 **Philosopher!:** as there is no query, ' Philosopher ' seems to be in scornful apposition to Physician.

127 19 **peep and botanise:** another of the poet's resentful views of the wrong spirit in Science (*cf*. 45.28).

129 54 **Hath been an idler:** the line may be applied to Wordsworth's own outward circumstances; but, clearly, he triumphs in the vindication of the poet's life.

TINTERN ABBEY

129 — Written in 1798 and published in *Lyrical Ballads*. In a note dictated to Miss Fenwick Wordsworth says:

> No poem of mine was composed under circumstances more pleasant for me to remember than this. I began it upon leaving Tintern, after crossing the Wye, and concluded it just as I was entering Bristol in the evening, after a ramble of four or five days with my sister. Not a line of it was altered, and not any part of it written down till I reached Bristol.

The poem is of vital importance for an understanding of Wordsworth's maturing faith, of his change from young passion

for nature to a haunting comprehension of the lovely universe
that holds 'the still, sad music of humanity.' The senses have
given nurture to imagination; and imagination grows to a living
soul. The poem should be read as a distinct forerunner to the
Immortality Ode, where the loss of youth's avidity is passionately
acknowledged. The *Ode to Duty* is a link between the two, in
accepting peaceably the answerability to universal law as something
greater than individual freedom.

The reading of *Tintern Abbey* may be facilitated by observation
of the following sections:

Lines.
1–22 The scene that is revisited.
22–35 The debt of purification owed, in pensive mood, to that scene.
35–57 From purification to a mysterious exaltation, in which is
    revealed a harmony beyond the fretful fever of the world.
58–83 Memory recalls the senses' first appetite for natural beauty.
83–102 Chastened mood has brought sympathy and a deeper
    wisdom: the soul grows in perception of a harmony that
    embraces human fate and natural beauty, both subject to
    spiritual force.
102–111 Confirmation, therefore, of faith in nature.
111–159 The poet's intimate sympathy with his sister: similar unfold-
    ing of her nature shall confirm their understanding.

129 1 **Five years have past:** *i.e.* since summer 1793.
129 4 **inland murmur:** Wordsworth here gave a footnote:

The river is not affected by the tides a few miles above Tintern . . .

130 25-27 The parallel with ' Daffodils,' 52.19-22, will be clear.
130 28 **along the heart:** *cf.* 4.5 for this use of ' along.'
132 106-107 **both what they half create, and what perceive:**
cf. **30.**16-17 and **124.**11-12. Wordsworth adds a note:

The line has a close resemblance to an admirable line of Young's,
the exact expression of which I do not recollect.

The passage occurs in *Night Thoughts*, vi, 417, etc.:

In senses, which inherit earth, and heavens;
Enjoy the various riches nature yields;
Far nobler! *give the riches they enjoy;*

Take in, at once, the landscape of the world,
At a small inlet, which a grain might close,
And half create the wondrous world they see.
Our senses, as our reason, are divine.

(The italics are mine.—Ed.)

ODE TO DUTY

134 — Written in 1805, on the model of Gray's *Ode to Adversity*, as Wordsworth points out, referring Gray's work to the model of Horace's ' Ode to Fortune.'

The Latin motto was added by Wordsworth in 1827. ' Now in counsel I am not wise, yet not only am I enabled to act aright but, thanks to my training, I am not able to do other than act aright.' This is taken, with slight adaptation, from Seneca, Epistle cxx.

For the main thought see note above, introducing *Tintern Abbey*. The death of his brother John had impressed Wordsworth for ever with a deeper sense of the inexorable hand of fate (*cf.* note upon *Elegiac Stanzas*, **126**). They had shared their love of the dales. John had died in duty to a stern profession, while William could stray ' in smoother walks.' Nevertheless the surrender to control is by the poet's own independent choice (*cf.* stanza 5). For resignation, compare the *Immortality* **Ode**; for submission to limitation, *cf.* Sonnet " Nuns fret not," p. **72.**

136 45-6 An echo of Gray's *Progress of Poesy*, ll. 5-6.

136 53 **made lowly wise :** cf. *Paradise Lost*, VIII, 173, ' Be lowly wise.'

ODE ON INTIMATIONS OF IMMORTALITY

137 — This poem was finished in 1806. " Two years at least," says Wordsworth, " passed between the writing of the first four stanzas and the remaining part." From entries in his sister's Journal it appears that the Ode was begun as early as 1802, in the same week as *My Heart Leaps Up* (p. 37), lines from which are here used as a motto.

" Nothing was more difficult for me in childhood," says the poet, " than to admit the notion of death as applicable to my own being. . . . It was not so much from feelings of animal vivacity that *my* difficulty came as from a sense of the indomitableness of the Spirit within me. I used to brood over the stories of Enoch and Elijah, and

almost to persuade myself that, whatever might become of others, I
should be translated, in something of the same way, to heaven."

(He then instances the 'abyss of idealism,' quoted in Introduction, xxxi.)

The Ode must be read in the light of foregoing poems. Both
the *Cuckoo* (p. 55) and *My Heart Leaps Up* (p. 37) proclaim the
illumination of childhood. *We are Seven* sets forth a child's
reluctance to imagine death. *Tintern Abbey* shows passion for
nature chastened and turned to vision. The *Ode to Duty* intro-
duces a sense of outer criterion and control. The Ode is now
presented in definite envisagement of glory departed, but it
surpasses the *Tintern* poem in majesty of aspiration, reaching
out as it does, not only to a sense of universal spirituality but
to 'Intimations of Immortality.' If the word 'Intimations' be
not lost from sight, the theme need not become controversial, not
to say heretical, as Wordsworth feared when he denied positive
doctrine of prenatal state (*cf*. Introduction, xxxiv). He is offering neither doctrine nor argument, but feelings of mysterious
continuity—in fact, intimations of immortality:

> We feel that we are greater than we know— (89.14).

(Notes of the following sections may prove helpful
in the study of this poem)

1-18   The Poet faces the fact that Nature, though still lovely,
        no longer brings to him the radiance of his youthful
        rapture.

19-35 Amid the gaiety of Spring, his grief is a reproach to him.
        He seeks to renew his faith, that he may answer the
        call to exultation.

36-57 Figures of joy and of innocence abound. And yet, con-
        templation, focussed upon individual objects, tells of
        a glory departed.

58-76 Sense of a prior state of existence, whose clear vision,
        however, fades with growing manhood.

77-84 Nature offers intrinsic joys in compensation for that
        greater loss.

85-107 The child becomes an actor: first he imitates life's
        routine in miniature, and then he passes to adult
        complexities, still acting.

108-132 The direct vision and wisdom of childhood extolled : the child bears with him a sense of Immortality (*cf.* l. 64), but he is doomed to change vision for convention.

133-138 Yet blessing remains from the fleeting sublimity.

138-151 Praise, not only for ' the simple creed of childhood,' but for the challenge proceeding from awakened thought (*see* note on ll. 145-6).

152-171 The primary affections are still the groundwork and nurture of our questioning thought : they are the ' master-light ' in which our seeing grows strong enough to hold assured vision of our part in Immortality.

172-190 The glad sights of Spring are, then, welcomed with profound joy, though consciousness of human suffering has replaced youth's exuberance by steady insight and the power of sympathy.

191-207 The Poet has kept faith with the loveliness of Nature, whose influence now takes another, more sombre way to his heart, and is the stronger and more intimate by contemplation. His deepest thought is of Nature's beauty, fraught with the sense of humanity, her child and habitant.

138 21 **tabor :** a small drum. The term is unexpected here ; but tabors were used in country dances.

138 28 **the fields of sleep :** opinion varies as to whether this phrase is meant allegorically or literally. Taken with the preceding line, it seems likely to refer to the actual fields, which could ' sleep,' *cf.* 53.5.

139 58 This new stanza re-opens the poem. *See* note above introducing the Ode ; also Introduction, xxxiv-xxxvi, where the thought is briefly discussed.

140 86 **A six years' Darling :** Professor Garrod thinks that Wordsworth had in mind Hartley Coleridge (*cf.* Footnote, Introduction, xxxv).

140 103 " **humorous stage** " : apparently an allusion to the famous "Seven Ages of Man" passage in *As You Like It*, II, vii.

141 110 **best Philosopher :** this section exalts the figure of the child. Coleridge thought that the exaltation went too far (*Biographia Literaria*, xxii).

141 121-24 The lines in brackets were omitted by Wordsworth in deference to the views of Coleridge. Line 117 was then

introduced, where the darkness of the grave applies metaphoric-
ally to our groping ignorance.

142 **143** **Not for these:** 'these' refers to 'Delight and liberty,
the simple creed of Childhood.'

142 **145-46** $\left\{\begin{array}{l}\text{But for those obstinate questionings} \\ \text{Of sense and outward things}\end{array}\right\}$: following
upon the 'abyss of idealism' passage (*cf.* introductory note above
and Introduction, xxxi), Wordsworth says:

> In later periods of life I have deplored, as we all have reason to do,
> a subjugation of an opposite character, and have rejoiced over the
> remembrances, as is expressed in the lines 'Obstinate Questionings.'

Mere reference to Wordsworth's 'own note' does not seem to
me helpful. When he says "As is expressed" it is hard to see
what 'subjugation' is expressed, and "the remembrances" is
a singularly vague expression. As far as I can see the 'subjugation' was to things of the sense (Mr Read points to Wordsworth's heaping up mountains of realism in order to banish the
abyss of solipsism); then, when the things of sense became over-
whelmingly real ('For nature then . . . To me was all in all,'
Tintern, **131.**72), the divine spirit in the man rebelled and set up
'obstinate questionings.' Thus it is that the

> High instincts before which our mortal Nature
> Did tremble like a guilty Thing surprised

are one with the more youthful premonitions of those instincts,
e.g. 'unknown modes of being' (**8.**37), 'sounds of indistinguish-
able motion' (**5.**23), 'inward agitations' (**15.**46), 'shadowy
things' (**21.**16).

142 **148-49** *cf.* 'unintelligible world,' **130.**40.

143 **174** *cf.* **138.**21; reiteration of this unexpected effect.

144 **206** **To me the meanest flower:** not natural beauty merely,
but wonder at existence itself, fraught with human fate, moves
the poet thus.

SOME SUGGESTIONS FOR ESSAYS AND DISCUSSION

1. What general emotions arise in Wordsworth from contemplation of individual things or men?

2. Wordsworth's optimism.

3. Give marked instances of feeling in Wordsworth's poetry heightened by metrical effect.

4. " Wordsworth's principle is that nothing is mean in nature." —(Elizabeth Barrett.)

5. Wordsworth's patriotism.

6. " The object contemplated is suddenly released from the tie of custom and becomes the source of a mysterious spiritual exaltation."—(Garrod.)

7. " It was not for passionless calm that he preferred the scenes of pastoral life."—(Pater.)

8. Discuss Wordsworth's attitude to children.

9. With what justice can it be said that Wordsworth's style resembles Milton's?

10. Comment on any passages in Wordsworth exact enough for police-court evidence.

11. Wordsworth's pathos is an " unmitigated, hard pathos, beyond the reach of sentimental palliatives."—(Raleigh.)

12. The effects of storm upon Wordsworth's imagination.

13. " It would really be easier to make out against Wordsworth a charge of excessive tolerance than a charge of excessive rigidity. A beggar is the sort of person he likes."—(Bradley.)

14. " It is true he was never humble."—(Harper.) Upon what evidence can this statement be refuted?

15. Major and minor contrasts in Wordsworth's poems.

16. " Wordsworth had not the faintest wish to see his countrymen the lords of human kind, nor is there anything vulgar in his patriotism: but there *is* ' pride in his port and defiance in his eye.' "—(Bradley.)

17. " He has much conventional sentiment."—(Pater.)

18. In what passages does Wordsworth conspicuously depart from his theory of humble diction ?

19. Speaking of the passage 14.31-37, Professor Bradley says : " Everything here is natural, but everything is apocalyptic." What passages answer to this description, and why ?

20. " This vast domain of perceptions and feelings he treated with something like the self-restraint, respect, and fidelity with which men of science investigate the material universe."— (Harper.)

21. " To him every natural object seemed . . . to be capable of a companionship with man."—(Pater.)

22. Compare Wordsworth's poetical product with the prose counterparts (by Dorothy Wordsworth, etc.) instanced in the *Notes*.

23. " . . . his consciousness apprehends things in a fashion essentially super-normal."—(Garrod.)

24. " Might, wisdom, joy, peace, these were not qualities projected by the imagination of man into a lifeless universe, but qualities that exist outside of man, and may pass into his life, if only he will be quiet and will attend."—(Raleigh.)   How is this belief represented in Wordsworth's work ?

25. Of the *Affliction of Margaret* Swinburne says : " Its idyllic effect is not heightened but impaired by the semi-dramatic form of narrative."   Discuss this statement with reference to Wordsworth's lack of plot.

26. What does Wordsworth mean by " Wise passiveness " (43.24) ?   Discuss fully with examples.

27. Discuss Wordsworth's attitude to old age.

28. " We to-day, more than 130 years afterwards, are still writing poetry in the tradition then established [at Alfoxden]." —(Read.)

29. To Wordsworth the ' Leech-gatherer ' (p. 108) is far more than a ' man poking in ponds with a stick.'—How ? and why ? and what other figures have similar effect on his mind ?

30. " In the airy building of the brain, a special day or hour even, comes to have for him a sort of personal identity, a spirit or angel given to it."—(Pater.)

A GUIDE TO READING

The following are some of the sources to which any serious student of Wordsworth must remain deeply indebted. I hope that my remarks, though necessarily brief, may help the reader to choose the angle from which to complete his own views.

A. Main Sources

The Complete Poetical Works:

> Edited by Edward Dowden (Aldine Edition, 1892, 7 vols.).
> Edited by Nowell C. Smith (Methuen, 1908, 3 vols.).
> Edited by Thomas Hutchinson (1 vol., Oxford, 1913, etc.).

> The handiest edition, most easily obtainable, is the last-named. All have profound scholarship, correcting previous editions, chief of which was that by William Knight.

The Prelude: Variorum Edition by Ernest de Sélincourt (Oxford, 1916).

> Besides unique scholarship upon hitherto unpublished sources, there is here an invaluable fund of criticism and notes.

Prose Works: Edited by Alexander B. Grosart (3 vols., Moxon, 1876).

> These volumes, of which the third contains the celebrated notes dictated by the aged poet to Miss Fenwick, are out of print. Main sections, however, are contained in the next volume named below.

Wordsworth's Literary Criticism, Ed. Nowell C. Smith (Oxford, 1905).

Letters of the Wordsworth Family, Ed. W. Knight (3 vols., Ginn, 1907). Out of print, but obtainable in a good library.

The Journals of Dorothy Wordsworth, Ed. W. Knight (Macmillan, new edition, 1924).

B. Contemporary Accounts and Criticism

Coleridge: *Biographia Literaria.* Especially Chapters iv, xiv,
    xvii-xxii.
                Biographia Epistolaris.
Hazlitt: *The Spirit of the Age (Wordsworth).*
         Winterslow (My First Acquaintance with Poets).
De Quincey: *Literary Reminiscences.*

> The first three works above-named deal with the poetry, the
> other two with the personality of Wordsworth. Many personal
> reminiscences also occur in :

H. Crabb Robinson: *Selections from Remains,* Ed. Edith Morley,
    and entitled *Blake, Coleridge, Wordsworth, Lamb, Etc.*
Aubrey de Vere: *Essays Chiefly on Poetry,* Vol. I, Chaps. iii
    and iv, on the Poetry; Vol. II, Chap. xv, Recollections.
Joseph Cottle: *Early Recollections.*

> Concerns mainly Wordsworth and Coleridge and *Lyrical
> Ballads.* By a proud publisher.

C. Biography and Later Criticism

Life: *William Wordsworth,* by George McLean Harper (Murray).

> First issued in 1916, the most complete history of the poet,
> stronger, however, in biography than in criticism. (*Cf.* John Bailey
> " A Mistaken View of Wordsworth " in *The Continuity of Letters,*
> Oxford, 1923.)

  Wordsworth, by **F. W. H.** Myers (English Men of Letters
    Series).

> Has deep regard for Wordsworth's moral and mystical values.
> Neglects the lyrical poems somewhat.

  The Early Life of Wordsworth, 1770-98, by Emile Legouis
    (Dent).

> Refers the poet's work unerringly to the influences that life,
> men, and books had upon his thought. A masterpiece of poised
> investigation.

Critical Works :

  Matthew Arnold, *Essays in Criticism* (2nd Series), Ch. v.

> Arnold laid stress on Wordsworth's originality and freshness,
> perhaps at the cost of his deeper traits of mystic imagination.

Swinburne, *Miscellanies* (fifth, on Byron and Wordsworth).

Swinburne rejects Arnold's comparison of Byron, and, with catholic choice of instances, asserts Wordsworth's grandeur and sublimity.

A. C. Bradley, *Oxford Lectures on Poetry* (*Wordsworth*).

Restores the mystic side neglected by Arnold. In a comparatively short space the difficult, brooding Wordsworth is wonderfully portrayed.

W. Pater, *Appreciations* (*Wordsworth*).

Written as long ago as 1874, a short essay with most sensitive insight and valuation.

G. Saintsbury, *History of English Prosody*, Vol. III, Ch. ii, for Wordsworth's metrical art.

A. Beatty, *William Wordsworth, His Doctrine and Art in their Historical Relations* (*Wisconsin*).

Specialist writing for specialist students. Close research on the poet's 18th-Century reading.

O. Elton, *Wordsworth*.
C. H. Herford, *Wordsworth*.

These two books assess Wordsworth's position in relation to the English tradition in literature. Professor Elton's book is the more critically genial of the two. Professor Herford's *The Age of Wordsworth* should also be consulted as the best concise general survey of the period. Also :

E. Dowden, *Studies in English Literature*, 1789-1877 (Ch. ii, The Transcendental Movement and Literature).

A. N. Whitehead, *Science and the Modern World* (Lowell Lectures, 1925).

Chapter v, 'The Romantic Reaction,' has striking tribute to Wordsworth from a modern scientist.

Herbert Read, *Wordsworth* (Clark Lectures, Cambridge, 1929-30).

Most modern of essays on the poet. In handling Wordsworth's character there is a vein of pitying psycho-analysis that should be taken with a grain of 'Habeas Corpus,' lest Wordsworth be condemned in absence ; but the tenacious examination of the poetry is inspired by veneration and insight.

H. W. Garrod, *Wordsworth*.

Chapters that show in small space a vigorous joy of exact scholarship. Both the last-named books offer, in widely different ways, an antidote to the appreciatory glamour that sometimes invades Professor Harper's big work.

W. Raleigh, *Wordsworth* (Publ. Arnold).

To my mind, the best single appreciation of Wordsworth. Mentioned last with a confession that I happened to read it last, when much of this book was in type. It is most wise, sane and generous.

There are many other works on Wordsworth written with particular view-point, *e.g.* Viscount Grey's Engl. Assoc. Booklet on *The Prelude*; Rawnsley's *Reminiscences* from Dalesmen; A. V. Dicey's *The Statesmanship of Wordsworth*; Catherine Maclean's *Dorothy and William Wordsworth*; and those readers who like an intimacy of Poetry and Topography will find a vigorous, full book in Eric Robertson's *Wordsworthshire*.